Spare the Rod

Love

the *Child*

ANNE B. GIELISSE, MA, ARNP, CNS

authorHOUSE®

About the Author

Anne B. Gielisse, MA, ARNP, CNS, a mother and grandmother, is a clinical nurse specialist in psychiatry and mental health, a marriage and family counselor, and a family and divorce mediator.

SPARE THE ROD LOVE THE CHILD is based on her experience of counseling individuals, couples, and families that spans more than thirty years. A mother and grandmother herself, she has a great deal of respect and empathy for parents.

Growing up in a family of nine children, Anne became interested in working with families and children early on. She studied nursing at the Boston Children's Hospital and worked as a nurse for several years. Once her own children reached adolescence, she went back to school to obtain a graduate degree in counseling and education with additional graduate work in couples and family therapy. She is committed to helping families provide safer, more loving homes for their children.

AuthorHouse™
1663 Liberty Drive
Bloomington, IN 47403
www.authorhouse.com
Phone: 1-800-839-8640

Published by AuthorHouse 01/22/2015

ISBN: 978-1-4969-5846-4 (sc)
ISBN: 978-1-4969-5845-7 (e)

If We Are To Reach Real Peace
In This World,
We Shall Have To Begin
With The Children.

MAHATMA GANDHI

Dedicated to

My daughters and my granddaughter
And all families and children everywhere

Acknowledgments

I thank my family for encouraging my interest in families; my daughters and my granddaughter for their loving support and creative assistance; Peter J. Gielisse, PhD and James S. Ackerman, PhD for editing; my teachers and friends who have assisted me in making this book a reality; and my cat for her unconditional love.

Contents

FOREWORD

I was a young teenager when my family arrived on the shores of the United States of America. Refugees from war-torn Europe, we had lost our home and most of our material possessions. My parents came with six children, much anticipation, and little else. Soon, three more little ones joined our ranks.

It was a challenging time for us. To this day I don't know how my parents managed to start over in a place so different from that of their origins, with nine children. They made mistakes. There were disappointments, there was much stress. They were fearful, yet I never saw them abdicate to fear. And we always kept on *loving* one another. We had that sense of family.

I am intrigued by my parents' approach to raising us. Yes, as a teenager and young adult, I was critical of my mother and father. Why didn't they do this or that better, and why didn't they tell us they loved us! Yet somehow we all knew that they did love us. When the world seemed uncaring and less than impressed with our talents, we could count on being received with open arms when we returned home. Throughout all the tough breaks that we experienced, it was the sense of being wanted, of being part of that clan which gave us the will to survive and grow.

When I became a mother, I was not yet a family therapist. Therefore, like most parents, I learned my skills on the job. I made many mistakes, and learned from them. In the process, I became fascinated with the structure and functioning of the human family. Already a nurse, I went back to college and on to graduate school in order to acquire more knowledge. I became a counselor, educator, and family therapist.

Over the years, I have guided numerous individuals, couples, families, and children of all ages. As I myself have continued to grow spiritually, something beautiful has happened. I have come to realize that the *essence* of mothering and fathering, *the* most important parenting skill, is love, unconditional love. I have also learned that, while we all possess the talent to love without conditions, few are born with that expertise in place. The good news is that this ability can be learned.

What do you need to do to learn unconditional loving? Let me be your guide. Let me teach you how to love in that fashion. And when you have mastered that skill, I will show you how to guide children with that kind of love.

And remember: children come to us on loan so that we may guide them with love and give them a good start in life.

Children Are
Our Most Valuable Natural Resource.

HERBERT HOOVER

INTRODUCTION

WE DO NOT OWN OUR CHILDREN

Children come to us on loan so that we may love them and give them a good start in life. That's it! They are not here to serve us, to make us feel good, or to make up for our shortcomings. Our role is to hold up the light, to show them the way. In other words, we are here to guide them with love, until they become adults. A responsibility of great magnitude indeed! For we prepare our offspring for a life of which we have no knowledge, for a time which we may never see. There is much that we can give them to ease their path, but what matters most is love, *unconditional love* that accepts and respects the child without judgment, without conditions. When that love is present on a sustained basis throughout childhood, youngsters thrive. It gives them the opportunity to acquire a healthy self esteem and to learn to respect others as well as themselves.

There are many types of families. Humanity, in its drive for diversity, has developed a multitude of religious preferences. Is it surprising that we would be equally creative in the expression of the very foundation of society, the family? Married, single; nuclear, extended; gay, straight; adoptive, or step families all can give to their youngsters that crucial ingredient which they must have to thrive, *love*. How their clan is put together matters little to children. The only concern of any importance whatsoever is that they have one or more caring adults who give them support and, most of all, unconditional love.

When they function well, families extend to children what no other institution in our society has been able to impart, a sense of knowing that they are wanted. This is the foundation of self esteem. It is that precious something that spawns the belief in ourselves, which gets us through even the most turbulent waters that life can present. In this world, filled with uncertainty and doubt, there is one flagship, the family, which can cast a bright beacon of light on the uncharted waters ahead.

In my experience, most of those who care for children yearn to be more loving toward them. Yet some don't know how to do that. They can't accept themselves or any one else without judgment. How, then, can they love children without conditions? And how can youngsters learn about unconditional love from adults who don't know how to love themselves?

SPARE THE ROD LOVE THE CHILD will show you a path into the domain of unconditional loving. The adventure begins with the first step: honoring and loving you, yourself, no strings attached, as a son or daughter of the Creator. Next, you will enter the world of the child, where you will discover the mental, emotional and spiritual needs of boys and girls during every phase of childhood. This will help you to understand youngsters better, so that you may become more accepting and loving toward them. Once introduced to that art, you will have the opportunity to learn how to guide children with love.

This book shows how to meet the needs of boys and girls of all ages, set limits, and discipline, with unconditional love, at every stage of development. The final chapter explains how you can maintain a healthy relationship with your offspring once they are grown, and how you can meet your own needs when they leave home.

Helpful exercises give you the opportunity to apply your new skills to your situation. This activity gives you the opportunity to express yourself and to help release new information into the data base of your mind.

SPARE THE ROD LOVE THE CHILD is written for parents, grandparents, teachers, child care and health professionals, neighbors, public servants, business people, anyone who works with, cares about, or is affected by children. It explains how everyone in the community can use the power of love to be more supportive to the basic building block of our society, the *family*. This book will assist you in learning to love yourself so that you can set appropriate boundaries and limits; and in teaching children to accept and love themselves, in order to help them grow into caring, balanced adults, who will pass along the ability to love unconditionally to *their* offspring.

Since this is a workbook with exercises and activities, it will be helpful to keep a journal available for your feelings, thoughts, and plans.

Now, gentle reader, it is time to begin your journey. Enjoy it, and walk in peace with love and light!

ONE

Parenting with Love

Ah kids!
We were all children once.
How soon we do forget!

A FAMILY IN DISTRESS

John and Mary have two children. Nancy is eleven, Mike nine years of age. John, a salesman, currently finds himself working more and more hours only to sell less and less. His wife, Mary, used to stay at home to care for the children. Now she works three part-time jobs as a bookkeeper, to enable her family to keep up their lifestyle. Both parents come home late from work. Since the family cannot afford after-school child care, Nancy and Mike are left on their own for several hours, after the school bus drops them off at home.

Mom and Dad told Nancy to look after Mike. But Mike, only two years younger than Nancy, refuses to accept her authority over him. When Nancy tells him to do his chores, he yells, "You're just my sister, you can't tell me what to do!", and runs off to join his friends in the streets.

Nancy, frustrated, complains to her parents. "Mike won't listen to me!" But they do not hear her. "We work hard all day to put food on the table for you. The least you two can do is to stop fighting" they exclaim.

Nancy gets angry. "I'll show them" she says to herself. When she finds out that Mike and his friends are sniffing glue, she does not tell her parents.

"They'll just blame me again," she rationalizes.

John and Mary learn about the glue sniffing when the principal of Mike's school calls to tell them that Mike has been suspended. Blaming Nancy, they yell at her. "You should have taken better care of him! You're both grounded for two months!"

Nevertheless, Mike and Nancy are still on their own after school, and they continue to do as they please. Nancy, feeling over-burdened with responsibility, is now hurt as well as angry. "I do everything around here and nobody cares about me" she sobs. Soon, friends invite her to

1

smoke cigarettes and drink some alcohol. "At least somebody likes me" she tells herself as she joins them.

WHAT HAS GONE WRONG IN THIS FAMILY?

This scenario and variations thereof are being repeated with ever greater frequency in our society, regardless of the economic or social position of the family. Parenting has become incredibly complex. Caught between unrealistic expectations on one hand, and the effects of peer pressure on their children on the other, fathers and mothers feel squeezed to their limits. Like a voracious virus, this kind of stress eats away at parents and children alike.

Emotional stress is not confined to the home. It quickly spreads to the workplace, where it translates into "job stress". If it is not dealt with, it can end up costing employers, and all of us, a great deal of money and much more. The effects of unrelieved tension in the work force, in terms of costly errors, decrease in motivation, increased illness, depression, panic attacks, accidents, burn-out, and employee turnover, affect all of our society. The damages, emotionally, mentally, physically, and economically, are staggering. The source is rarely recognized. We currently spend more time and money putting Band-Aids on stress and feeding people pills than we do on doing something about the root cause of the problem.

The situation is compounded by the fact that the skills for mothering and fathering, the most important jobs on Earth, are rarely taught in schools. We learn from observing and imitating our parents, who made their share of mistakes. They had no formal education for this critical work, either!

Meanwhile, technological advances are forcing societal change with lightning speed. Traditional values are discarded before new ones have a chance to evolve and take their place. As a consequence, much of what our parents taught us appears obsolete by the time the next generation rolls around. The world in which we function is very different from that in which our elders lived. In turn, we are preparing our offspring for a future that we can barely envision.

SINGLE MOTHERS AND FATHERS

The dilemma for the solo parent is even more acute. Lacking the support of an adult partner, the single mother or father often has to carry the entire burden of child rearing. Custody fights and other disagreements with the non-custodial parent can make this a crushing ordeal. The resulting stress on these men and women cannot be imagined by those who have not walked this road. It takes its toll physically, emotionally, mentally and economically, not only of the adults, but of the children as well.

STEP-PARENTS FACE ADDITIONAL CHALLENGES

Fairy tales and novels vividly illustrate how difficult it is to step into the shoes of the absent father or mother. Today, with support by extended families almost nil, this has become an even greater challenge. What is expected of you? How do you behave toward step-children? Should you discipline them? How do you talk about your fears? Most people don't. They believe that they should know the answers and blame themselves if they don't. Wanting nothing more than to be accepted by their partners' youngsters, step-mothers and fathers often find themselves rejected instead. When biological parents speak unfavorably of their children's step-parents, they complicate the situation even more.

WHAT HAPPENS TO THE CHILDREN?

While mothers and fathers are over-stressed, it is their offspring that suffer the most. Often a self-reinforcing cycle of stress develops that turns all too easily into abuse. Causing much pain and fear for the youngsters, this situation hurts the adults as well. In my counseling practice I have met very few parents who abused their children because they wanted to injure them. Most adults punish excessively when they are under the influence of stress and/or the drug or alcohol they are consuming in the effort to relieve the stress. Any abuse that they may have suffered in their childhood will tend to pre-dispose them to becoming abusive themselves.

How does that work? Let's check it out.

The Stress-Abuse Cycle

Parent feels abused by stress

Child gets into more trouble

Parent over-punishes the child

Parent becomes more abusive

Child becomes rebellious

Overly-strained parents, hurting from old wounds and lacking parenting skills, may put stress on their children by blaming them, yelling at them, or even beating them. Treated this way, youngsters develop more behavioral problems; which increases the pressure on the parents; who then punish even more harshly. The youngsters' problem behaviors escalate; and thus *the cycle repeats itself.*

It is a great tragedy that child abuse is so rampant in our "civilized" society. Spouse abuse, equally disastrous, harms the witnessing children as much as it does the adult victim. What do these circumstances say about us?

WHAT KIND OF LEGACY ARE WE PASSING ON?

Always at risk of being abused emotionally, physically, or sexually, children may end up losing their childhood, their innocence, and their peace of mind. Being small and vulnerable, they make easy prey for human predators. As a consequence, they may become depressed, suffer panic attacks, and/or develop dissociative disorders, obsessions, and compulsions. They may turn to substance abuse, become involved in crime, or commit suicide. If not worked through, these challenges follow their survivors into adulthood. Then the abuse may be passed along to the next generation.

HELPING OUR FAMILIES

Numerous books, workshops, and talk shows have addressed the issue. National, state, and local governments are searching for solutions. Yet the *crucial* ingredient, *love*, is often overlooked. Polarization and prejudice are fueled by this deficiency. If we want to make a lasting impact, we need to start caring about one another.

All families are *our* families, just as the community in which we live is our community. The problems affecting other families touch us as well. It is said that love can move mountains. Once we realize that the problems encountered by all families are *our* problems; and once we, all of us, join *hearts, souls, and hands* with those families, with love, then we will begin to find the solutions which we are so desperately seeking.

LOVE BEGINS IN THE HOME

Love starts with fathers and mothers caring for their children unconditionally and telling them daily that they love them. Love is the single most effective parenting skill. It is the *heart and soul* of mothering and fathering. Guiding and disciplining children with unconditional love is crucial to the unfolding and the development of their personalities. More essential than all the material comforts which money can buy, this kind of loving cannot be bought. It comes from the heart and needs to be disbursed freely and without reservation.

HOW TO SHOW CHILDREN THAT YOU LOVE THEM

There is a dilemma. Parents seem to be afraid to love their children unconditionally. Many don't know how. Few adults have been raised with that kind of love. Thus they have not learned to love *themselves* without conditions. Love flows from the Creator into us. It is then up to us to accept and care for ourselves as we are, as part of His creation. Once we accomplish that, we are ready to pass that unconditional love on to our children. When we open our hearts to this love energy, it becomes an ever-moving stream, flowing from one heart into another. At first barely a trickle, it broadens into a creek that turns into a river, which empties into a vast ocean of love. Once started, the love force cannot be stopped.

The good news is that everyone can participate in this process ~ parents, children, relatives, friends, neighbors, tribes, nations, the entire planet. *All of us can love one another*. And all of us can learn to give loving sustenance to the cornerstone of our society, the family. Supported by this vast safety net, mothers and fathers can focus more readily on their primary task: channeling love to their children.

BEYOND THE NUCLEAR FAMILY

Long before there were cities and nations, people lived in tribal communities. Most tribes were supportive of their members. They provided for surrogate parenting to children whose parents were not available. Emotional and practical safety nets to assist families in difficult circumstances were firmly in place. Once humanity left tribal communities, we lost this connection with one another. Yet, we still depend upon each other, now more than ever.

What affects one of us, touches us all. If Mike becomes part of a gang of young criminals for lack of loving care, all of us are impacted, whether or not we are the direct target of the perpetrators. If Nancy continues to see alcohol and nicotine as her only friends and allows them to abuse her body, mind and spirit, the impact of her deteriorating health will go far beyond her and her family. Insurance companies increase their rates for all of us to pay for their losses, and governments keep raising taxes to finance hospitals, treatment programs, and prisons. Who do you suppose ends up paying those bills?? What about the loss of something far less concrete than money, but much more precious to humanity? How do you put a dollar sign on the *talents* of these children, talents perhaps never realized because we insist on staring at costs in terms of money alone? How do you figure the *real cost of* talent *lost* to society? And who pays for that?

I am posing many questions. Some of them I will answer. The solutions, however, must come from all of us joining together to participate in a task of the greatest importance, the *guiding of children with love;* for we are, indeed, *all one tribe.*

TWO

What Is Love?

Ever around you,
Love becomes yours,
Once you open your heart.

Unconditional love is the *divine spark* within us. It starts with the Creator and moves through all His creation, the two-legged and four-legged ones, those that fly, swim, or crawl, the plants, and the rock people. Love is our connection with the Creator, who always loves us as we are, without limits, without conditions. And it links us to *all our relations*, in other words, all that He has brought forth. The task for us is to open our hearts to His love and to let it flow from us into Grandmother Earth, each other, and all His creation. That is what life is about.

So you see, it's really quite simple. Then why do we make it so difficult? Perhaps it is because we look for love in the wrong places. Is it any wonder that it seems hard to find? And yet, it is there all around us, all the time. You too, can feel it, once you open your heart.

HOW DO YOU OPEN YOUR HEART?

First, welcome the love that the Creator offers you. Feel its presence around you. It is everywhere. Next, accept and love yourself. Then do the same for others, without judgment, without conditions. This sequence is crucial. In order to be able to *truly* love another, we need to love the Creator and ourselves first.

Something precious happens when we open our hearts to this kind of loving. We become compassionate and understanding. More ready to forgive ourselves and others, we let go of the need to own or change those whom we love. A new awareness takes root. We are able to feel our connection with Grandmother Earth and all our relations. Once we reach that point, we are able to *see*, as we never saw before, the wonder and beauty that is everywhere, all around us.

RECOGNIZING UNCONDITIONAL LOVE

Unconditional love starts in the heart and spreads from there throughout body, mind, and spirit. You'll feel it as a gentle radiance diffusing your entire system. While similar to the glow of being in love, it is also quite different. Independent from another person's love, unconditional love comes from inside, from that place deep within you that is your direct connection with God. It sharpens the senses. It is *healing* and it benefits you first and foremost, and then all those around you.

Take an honest look at yourself. Perhaps you already love something in a non-judgmental way. Work, material things, money, nicotine, alcohol, drugs, gambling, which one is it for you? Is it not better to *love people*, yourself included, without condition, and to use some *judgment* regarding the attachment to mere things? You have a choice: you can make a decision and throw an internal switch, to shift your loving to the living!

LOVING YOURSELF VERSUS SELF-INDULGENCE

Loving yourself has nothing to do with being selfish. As a matter of fact, there is no need for selfishness once we accept ourselves and others as we are. Start with giving yourself permission to love yourself. Let's try it.

Learning to Love Yourself

1. Set aside a time and place for yourself. Make sure that there are *no* interruptions.
2. Breathing deeply and slowly, become quiet. Take your time. Pay attention to the rhythm of your breath. Exhale every breath *very* slowly through your mouth.
3. Still breathing deeply and slowly, become aware of the presence of the Creator and His love that *always* surrounds you.
4. Notice that He is within you, as well as around you.
5. Love the divine presence, as you would someone of whom you are very fond.
6. Now accept yourself as you are AT THIS MOMENT, shortcomings, wrinkles, and all.
7. Say to yourself *I accept myself as I am*. Forgive yourself for being less than perfect.
8. Plan to do something positive for *you*, to give yourself a gift. Be aware that you are your own best friend.
9. Repeat this exercise at least once a day.
10. Write down your feelings and any insights in your journal.

LOVE AND FEAR

The absence of love is fear. Love is light, fear is darkness. Fear causes us to be indifferent, or non-caring, toward self or others. It underlies all negative feelings, such as anger, hurt, sadness, prolonged guilt, and shame. *It is destructive to hold on to those feelings.* They hurt us physically, emotionally, mentally, and spiritually. They can block our efforts to love ourselves. Let them go, replace them with love.

Since prolonged guilt is so prevalent in our society, let's start with forgiving yourself. This exercise is a reminder that whatever you hold against yourself is actually a distraction from the Light and the Creator. To bring yourself back, *refocus* on the Light. Remember, He has already forgiven you. Rather than wasting your energy on continuing to blame yourself, channel it into learning from your mistake. Repeat this exercise as often as you need it. It has only beneficial side effects!

Forgiving Yourself

1. Breathing deeply and slowly, become still.
2. Say out loud, so that the sound waves of your voice can reach your ears, making the message even more powerful: *I forgive myself for all distraction from the Light.*
3. Picture light, in whatever color presents itself to you, flowing toward you.
4. Surround yourself with that light.
5. Let the light flow into you, filling the place inside you from which you released the guilt.
6. Write down your feelings and thoughts in your journal.

THE IMPACT OF INDIFFERENCE

Indifference, the absence of caring, is experienced as rejection. As traumatic as the loss of a loved one, it hurts youngsters deeply. Children require the words *I love you*, they need to be held in a safe way. And when there is no one who is willing or able to assist them, no one to whom they can turn, children become terrified and feel abandoned. Not knowing how to help themselves, some numb their pain by repressing, or "stuffing" it.

Repressed negative feelings are stored in the body. As they build up, they prevent the free flow of love within the individual. Depression or chronic anxiety usually ensues. Pretty soon the body starts reacting with fatigue, allergies, headaches, proneness to accidents, or other physical problems. Due to the stress upon body, mind, and spirit, the child's immunity may become impaired, resulting in lowered resistance to infections, such as chronic colds, sore throats, etc. Some youngsters start shrinking from social contact, others develop behavior problems. Eventually, while still able to grow physically and mentally, they may stop maturing emotionally, especially when there is no relief from the trauma.

The good news is that stored feelings can be released. Once they are processed and let go, healing can take place. The flow of love energy is restored and emotional growth resumes. This process will be described in greater detail in a subsequent chapter.

THE IMPORTANCE OF LOVE

Youngsters require much love and support from everyone around them. It is frightening to be born helpless; it is scary to grow up in times of uncertainty and change. Be sure to provide a safe haven, acceptance, tenderness, respect, encouragement, and a supportive environment. Tell children that you *love* them, they need to hear it. Hug them daily. Teach them to learn from their mistakes, applaud even the smallest of successes. Children thrive when they can count on being loved unconditionally in a steady, balanced way.

TEACHING CHILDREN TO LOVE THEMSELVES

A major parental responsibility, teaching your offspring to love themselves is best carried out through example. Love yourself, and the little ones, who copy your behaviors, learn the first step toward loving themselves. When you, Mom and Dad, are a loving couple and demonstrate in word and deed that you love one another, your sons and daughters learn the basics of loving themselves, you, and others. When you treat yourself, each other, and your children, with respect, the youngsters learn to value and respect themselves, you, and other people. By accepting mistakes as *learning experiences* rather than failures, you mirror that ability to those who watch you. Once you forgive them, you will show your offspring how to forgive and love themselves.

SINGLE PARENTING

When Mom and Dad do not live together, they can still show their children that they care about the other parent by talking to and about each other respectfully. Making nasty comments about each other, refusing to pay child support, or engaging in destructive court battles, is not acceptable. These behaviors teach young people that it is OK to be unloving and disrespectful. Is that what you want them to learn? Forgiving each other, letting go of the need for revenge, and moving on emotionally once you have finished your grieving, make for a powerful way to model healthy love of self and others for your offspring.

It is totally possible to work things out amicably and in the best interest of your children. When one of my daughters and her husband decided to divorce, they experienced strong feelings of loss and grief. They recognized that these emotions blocked their ability to work things out in a way that would smooth the transition for their child. Therefore they worked through their feelings and improved their communication with each other. Together, they figured out how to honor their daughter's needs, while taking care of their own. Both have carefully avoided burdening their child with negative messages about each other.

Lovingly supported by her parents, my granddaughter has been able to work through her feelings of loss and grief to continue her emotional growth without interruption. Her parents have made sacrifices in the *highest interest of their child*. Their reward comes from knowing that she is healthy and happy now. This, in turn, has eased their own transition through this passage.

That is how unconditional loving works. Though there may be difficulties at first, situations are worked out in a win/win manner for everyone concerned. Cooperation prevails over competition. The common good and the needs of the child are made the highest priority. Thus any blockages have a chance to dissolve, so that the love energy can once again flow unimpeded.

THREE

About Children

To guide children,
Understand their needs.
To love children,
Show them you understand.

The needs of children have been studied from every angle, in recent times. Yet, though we know more about them now than we ever have, that knowledge is insufficiently utilized in the rearing of our offspring. How does that come about?

The answer is that information in and of itself does not suffice. Yes, knowing about the needs of children is important. Without understanding them, however, we are nowhere. How then do you get from knowing to comprehending? First care enough to search for the information, and then take the time to digest it. Next, apply the data to your child and add a large dose of love. Finally, show your youngster that you understand, by putting your knowledge into action on a full time basis. Once you have accomplished all that, you will be on the path of unconditional loving. Are you ready for that?

THE EMOTIONAL NEEDS OF YOUNGSTERS

When I asked my then ten-year-old granddaughter what children most need from their parents, she replied without hesitation, "Two things: tell parents to remember their childhood and how they wanted to be treated when they were kids, and tell them to spend more time with their kids."

I have listened to youngsters for many years, but the clarity and depth of their answers still give me goose bumps. They tell us what they need, when we take the time to listen. In her brief statement, my grandchild summed up the basic emotional needs of children of all ages: *love, respect, and nurturing*.

Boys and girls require love, respect and emotional and mental sustenance as much as they need food, sleep, and security. Demonstrate your love with touch, and express it in words, daily. Show respect by listening and communicating. Keep in mind that children cannot read your mind.

Nurture their intellects by answering their questions and letting them solve problems that they can handle. Hold them and console them when they hurt, praise them for their effort.

GUIDING CHILDREN WITH LOVE

Little ones require much holding and hugging in order to thrive. Yet many adults are fearful of touching youngsters, lest they be accused of sexual abuse. How do you walk this road? There is a way. It is called *safe touch*.

SAFE TOUCH

What is safe touch? It is non-sexual holding, hugging, and stroking. A good rule of thumb is to avoid contact with those parts of the bodies of girls or boys that are covered by a bathing suit, or swim trunks, respectively. Clearly, there are exceptions, when adults in parenting roles, or health care providers, need to cleanse the genitalia of youngsters, or provide medical treatments. When done for that purpose, in a respectful manner, and without sexual intent, it should not hurt the child.

THE CHALLENGES OF RAISING CHILDREN

Children ask so little of us. And yet, the more we learn about them, the more complex their care appears to become. Why do youngsters present such a challenge to most of us?

The answer is that the needs of adults and those of their offspring are often at cross purposes. For example, infants require much holding and touching for emotional reassurance. This is so crucial that those who are not held sufficiently cannot thrive. If the baby's mother or father, on the other hand, is still harboring anger about something that happened in their own childhood, he or she might feel suffocated by all this closeness and dependence. Bonding with the child will be difficult until the anger is released and let go. Negative feelings block the flow of love from parent to child. These emotions can be as toxic to the infant as the wrong kind of food. Adults need to learn to meet their own needs, even while providing for the children in their care. Mom and Dad can help themselves by releasing and letting go of their negative feelings. I will demonstrate how that is done.

RELEASING AND LETTING GO OF NEGATIVE FEELINGS

Grownups, for any number of reasons, often like to hold onto their anger, hurt, sadness, guilt, shame, frustration, and fears. Therefore, ask yourself first whether you are ready to relinquish your negative feeling, for nothing will happen until you are. If the answer is yes, first make the decision to do so, and then follow through with action as quickly as possible. Since emotions bind themselves to the body, you need to release them before you can let them go. The following exercise will show you how to do both. Use the *exact wording* as provided, to make sure that the part of you that is holding on can comprehend the message.

Releasing and Letting Go

1. Breathing slowly and deeply, become quiet.
2. Focus your heart and spirit on the Creator.
3. Say out loud: *I am releasing and letting go of . . .*
4. Fill in your feeling, such as anger, pain, or fear, but only one at a time.
5. Be sure to use the exact wording. You need to release before you can let go.
6. Allow yourself to feel the release. You will experience it physically as well as emotionally.
7. Repeat the process if you wish to let go of other feelings. If you are unable to release and let go, you may need to do further work on these issues. How that is done will be addressed in a subsequent chapter.
8. Write down your feelings and insights in your journal.

CHILDREN IN GROWN-UP SHOES.

Jack, the single father of Tammy and Eddie, had a rough childhood. He was emotionally and physically abused by his father. His mother was not strong enough to protect him. Recently divorced, Jack has custody of his children, Tammy, age 12, and Eddie, age 8 years. While struggling with the demands of single parenting, Jack is feeling overwhelmed by grief due to the ending of his marriage. When these feelings tap into the pain left from the abandonment that he experienced in his childhood, he becomes depressed and morose.

Tammy observes her father's sadness and hurt. She also misses her mother very much. Aching, she really wants to confide in her dad. But seeing his grief, she cannot bring herself to do that. "Poor dad" she thinks, and decides to bury her own agony in an effort to be supportive to him. She becomes a little mom to her father and brother. She cooks, cleans, and tends to Jack's emotional wounds.

In this situation, Jack and Tammy have switched roles. Tammy has become a nurturing parent to Jack. Her father, in making himself emotionally dependent on her, has relinquished his parental role. Whether he realizes it or not, he is taking out his anguish on his daughter. As a result, Tammy, only 12 years of age, has lost what was left of her childhood.

Parents, teachers, health care professionals, day care workers, any one who has not worked through their issues can fall into the trap of displacing their needs and emotions onto children. Since the adult is in a position of power, there is little that youngsters can do to protect themselves. This situation causes them much confusion, coupled with suffering and stress. Lacking the maturity to comprehend what is going on, they feel helpless and powerless. Some blame themselves. Others, realizing the unfairness of the situation, take out their anger on someone else.

Let's see then how you can learn to meet *your* needs.

LEARNING TO MEET YOUR OWN NEEDS

In order to be good enough as a father to Tammy and Eddie, Jack must work through his pain and abandonment issues. He also requires emotional support and a crash course in single parenting, so that he can move forward into his role as a father. To do all of this while he is in the middle of a crisis and trying his best to make a living, can be difficult. This is a good time for him to seek assistance from a family therapist.

How do you learn to take care of your emotional needs? It is not difficult to work through, release, and let go of your negative feelings, using the exercise that I taught you earlier in this chapter. Displacing needs and emotions onto others is a learned behavior. It can be unlearned and replaced with healthier habits. So, let's see how that is done.

Meeting Your Needs

1. Breathing deeply and slowly, become quiet.
2. Take an honest look at your life. Are you taking out any negative feelings on your children?

How do you do that? Write it down in your journal.

3. Admit to yourself the specific feeling involved in this situation.
4. Release it, using the previous exercise.
5. Say, out loud, *I am releasing and letting go of the need to be a burden to . . .*
6. Fill in the blank with the name of the child.
7. Forgive yourself for your mistake.
8. Fill the void with light and ask for guidance in learning to meet your own needs.
9. See yourself taking care of yourself without leaning on anyone.
10. Write down your feelings. Add what you plan to do to change the situation.

THE OTHER SIDE OF THE COIN: SMOTHERING.

Alex and Barbara have a good marriage, but Alex's career requires him to travel a great deal. They have decided that Barbara resign from her job in order to be a full time mother to their nine-year-old son David. Barbara misses her husband's emotional support when he is gone, and craves the fulfillment that her career used to give her. She hovers over David and becomes overprotective of him. All her time and energy are spent on catering to him. Not realizing that she is making him more and more dependent on her, she even does his homework for him. David, however, is beginning to resent her clinging ways. He attempts to pull away from her. Barbara, hurt, accuses him of not loving her. As a mother, she is unable to find the balance between loving and smothering, guiding and stifling, teaching and rescuing her son. Though unconsciously, she is taking out her feelings of loss and grief on her son.

Overly protecting children can cripple them emotionally. They become fearful and avoid taking risks. Growing up thinking that they are powerless, these youngsters learn to say *I can't*. Feeling that they are not allowed to err, or that they might hurt someone if they do, they do nothing. Or they look to someone else to take care of them. Once they become adults, they are often passive, avoid risk, and seem to fear success as much as failure.

Letting children make their mistakes, on the other hand, gives them the opportunity to learn from these learning experiences. This enables them to grow into confident adults. When babies learn to walk, they fall repeatedly, pick themselves up, and try again. Every fall teaches them something about becoming two-legged, so that, before long, they will be able to propel themselves forward in an upright position, step by small step. *Mistakes are but steps toward mastery.*

GUIDING YOUR CHILDREN WITH LOVE

How can you find the balance between neglect and smothering? The key is to *guide* children with unconditional love, i.e., love that knows no reservations and places no conditions, while you love yourself in that manner as well. The latter assures that you set the limits and boundaries that both you and your child need. The principles of this kind of loving are detailed below. Subsequent chapters will show you how to implement these objectives at every stage of your child's development.

RECIPE FOR UNCONDITIONAL LOVING

♥   Accept and respect the individuality and uniqueness of every child.
♥   Nurture youngsters emotionally and mentally, as well as physically.
♥   Tell them daily that you love them. Give them plenty of hugs and kisses.
♥   Avoid displacing your reaction to the stress in your life onto children.
♥   Take care of yourself. Release and let go of negative feelings as soon as possible.
♥   If your relationship with your spouse or partner is strained, work it out as quickly as you can.
♥   Avoid taking out your negative feelings on your offspring.
♥   Realize that boys and girls need limits and boundaries.
♥   Be honest.
♥   Respect the feelings of children. Behave toward them as *you* expect to be treated.
♥   Have age-appropriate expectations, but do not place more responsibilities on them than they are able to handle.

♥ Get professional help when you need it to help you accomplish these objectives.

♥ Remember that you do not own your sons and daughters. Children come to us so that we may raise them and teach them how to love. When this has been accomplished, when they are grown, we need to let go. Our job is done.

FOUR

Fathers, Mothers, And Others

Fathers and mothers,
And all those who care for children,
Need nurturing too.

Fathers, mothers, and all those that work with children have emotional needs too. They require a great deal of support from their spouses, extended family, friends, and neighbors; and from the community at large. As a matter of fact, your needs are quite similar to those of the ones in your charge; for you, like the rest of us, have a little child within you, no matter how old you are.

THE CHILD WITHIN YOU

You might think of your inner child as that part of you that holds all the innocence and wonder left from your childhood. It is also your creative, fun-loving self. It, too, requires unconditional loving, respect, and encouragement. Can you really rely on others to do that for you? Can you count on them to be there for you when you most need them? Probably not. You can, however, nurture yourself. In fact, that is the only way in which you can make sure that the little girl or boy inside you gets all the love she or he needs, all the time. Let's see how that is done.

Doing Loving Things for Yourself

1. Take a moment to thank yourself. Give yourself a pat on the back for doing something worthwhile, even if you did not do it well. It is truly the effort that counts.
2. Reflect on something that you can do for yourself, something loving. It does not have to cost money.
3. Plan how you will do it.
4. Write down your strategy in in your journal.
5. What is it like to plan to do something for yourself? Experience that feeling physically, as well as emotionally.

Write down your reactions.

6. Now carry out your plan! And have fun!

REACHING OUT TO YOUR INNER CHILD

If you haven't already had the experience, you might want to make closer contact with your child within. It pays to get to know that intuitive part of you. Intuition is like antennae extending from you that help you sense things before you can figure them out with your mind. We were all born with that gift. Many of us have been trained away from it, however, due to the emphasis on intellect in our educational systems.

Wouldn't you like to hone your intuitive ability? Let's see how you can open up the communication channels between you and your child within. When you pay attention to its needs, its love and support will flow back to you.

Making Contact with Your Inner Child

1. Make yourself comfortable in a secluded, quiet place.
2. Close your eyes and become still.
3. Focus on your breathing. With every gentle breath you take, exhale negative feelings and inhale the Creator's love for you.
4. Picture yourself as a child, at whatever age first comes to mind.
5. Mentally see yourself walking toward that child, and put your arms around it.
6. Take it on your lap, hold it close, and listen to what it wants to say to you.
7. Tell it that you love it, without conditions, and that you will do your best to protect it from being hurt again. Give it a long hug.
8. How did that feel? Write down your feelings and insights.

BECOMING PLAYFUL

Do you know how to play? I'm serious, do you? We all have the innate ability to play. If you have misplaced yours, watch children while they are at play. Notice that they enjoy it. Reconnect with your ability to play for the sake of your inner child, as well as the youngsters in your charge. Playing and creativity go hand in hand. They are an intricate part of childhood, and thus of your inner child. As we grow up, our ability to have fun is sometimes squelched by those who do not know better. Perhaps this has happened to you. This is a good time to get in touch with your feelings about that, so that you can release them and let them go.

Letting Go Of the Fear of Having Fun

1. Breathing deeply and slowly, become quiet.
2. Become aware of any troubling feeling that might prevent you from having fun (e.g. fear, anger, guilt, shame, sadness), then state the feeling out loud.
3. Let yourself experience the feeling, physically as well as emotionally.
4. Say, loud enough so that you can hear *I am releasing and letting go of* . . . (plug in the emotion).
5. Take a deep, cleansing breath, exhaling the negative feeling.
6. Inhale deeply, drawing into yourself love and light, to fill the void left by the release.
7. Take several deep breaths, letting go of negatives as you exhale; then let love and light flow into your body as you inhale.
8. How did that feel? Write down your emotions and any insights.

It was good to let go of this load, was it not? Be sure to replace whatever you release with love and light, lest other negative feelings creep into the void. This exercise may be repeated until you have released and let go of all the negative emotions about this issue.

CAUTION: If this exercise is uncomfortable to you, or if it is difficult for you to get in touch with or release these feelings, there may be a good reason. It may be frightening to your inner child to feel the pain associated with some childhood memories. If this is happening to you, be gentle with yourself. Don't push. It would be safer for you to process any painful childhood memories with a family therapist or counselor who is experienced in this type of therapy. He or she can assist you in dealing with your memories, so that they will not get in the way of your relationship with the children in your care.

Learning How to Work Playfully

"Work playfully?" I would have exclaimed a few years ago. Now I know that this is actually desirable. Those who are among the many that are too serious about work don't know what they are missing. And neither do their bosses. The fact is that you can do an excellent job, while doing it playfully. You will find yourself actually enjoying your work, and get it done with less effort. Best of all, you will be more creative and have more energy. By the way, have you noticed that this book was written in a playful manner?

How About Giving It a Try!

1. While you are at work on a task, any task, become aware of your feelings about the work. Write them down.
2. Observe your behavior while you are at work. Jot down your observations.
3. Review your notes. What do they tell you about yourself? Write down your reactions.

Fortunately we are never too old to learn. To do that, let us observe the authorities on play, children. Think about it, have you ever had to teach toddlers to have fun? They know how to do this intuitively. So, let's watch them.

Learning from the Experts

1. Watch small children while they are at play.
2. Observe their behaviors while they are playing by themselves.
3. Compare their behavior with your own work and play behavior.
4. Join the youngsters. Imitate their actions.
5. Write down your feelings.
6. Jot down what you learned.

Did you notice how absorbed young children become in play? They are as serious about it as we are about work, but in a much more fun-loving way. Have you ever heard of a child getting burned out from play? Write down your reactions.

HOW TO LOVE AND SUPPORT YOUR PARTNER'S INNER CHILD

When parents live together, they need to accept, love and support one another. You got together for love; now let that emotion grow within you and between you. Let go of the need to be judgmental. Show each other affection with hugs and caring touch. Nurture your relationship. Have fun together. Loving couples become loving parents.

Are there negative feelings between you that you can't work out? Do leftovers from past hurts keep intruding? Perhaps it is time to consult a counselor or family therapist, to work them through and let them go.

Tracy and Mark, married for several years, are talking about starting a family. Quickly, it becomes apparent that they disagree on a number of child raising issues. Tracy argues "But this is so important!" Mark comes back with "But I just see it another way!" as they both try to convince each other of their points of view. All at once they stop, look at each other and exclaim "What has happened to us?"

Point Of View

1. Invite your spouse or partner to join you for a discussion of your values (preferences, likes, dislikes, etc.).
2. Share your values with each other.
3. Listen with acceptance and an open heart.
4. Be honest. Avoid being critical.
5. Check out your assumptions about what your partner is saying, by asking for clarification.
6. Share your feelings about this exercise with each other.

Tracy and Mark decided to see a family therapist to help them work through their differences before attempting conception. In the process of therapy, they learned to accept each other where they are, and to reach consensus on important matters. They opened their hearts to unconditional love. As they grew in emotional closeness, their sexual relationship improved as well. They are now ready to help bring a new soul into this world.

THOSE WHO RAISE CHILDREN REQUIRE COMMUNITY SUPPORT

In order to provide children with the stable home environment which they require, those who parent children need stability in their own lives. Extended families, neighbors, cities, counties, states, and nations all are in the position to assist with this. Birds flock together for their protection. Animals support each other within their own families. For countless generations we used to do the same. It is time to do it once again, to assure OUR SURVIVAL.

There are many ways to support parents: classes in parenting skills and stress management; emotional support, especially in times of crisis and illness; understanding; empathy; and compassion; and financial assistance when it is needed. Rather than luxuries, these are necessities. They provide a safety net for our families.

Observe what the absence of this support has spawned: Teen pregnancies; spousal and child abuse; boys and girls dying for want of love and nurturing; crimes committed by youngsters. And now, children are maiming and killing children. Does anyone care? When we do not treasure our greatest resource, our young, when we put love of material goods and comfort before love of our offspring, what does that say about us as a society? When we turn away from the plight of a child, or a parent, can we still call ourselves human? Can we survive as a civilization?

Much can be done to assist mothers and fathers. If your children are grown, you can make yourself available to teach parenting skills or to baby sit. You might volunteer to tell stories to youngsters in our libraries, to do the shopping for busy parents, or to help with household chores and cooking. This is what neighbors used to do in times of need! Our world is still in need of this kind of cooperation. It is time that we realized that we are all family, whether related by blood lines or not. We are all brothers and sisters. What impacts our neighbors, affects us all in our global village.

FIVE

Padding Your Home with Love

Home's where your heart is,
It is said.
But what is IN your heart?

The home is where the action is, the place where children are raised. Birds lovingly make ready their nests for the arrival of their young. The division of labor, such as how the food will be collected, who will do the feeding, and how the young will be trained, is worked out well before the first chick peeks out of its shell. Humans in the Western world mostly overlook this step in their preoccupation with being in love. Yet, preparing for the arrival of offspring is as crucial for two-leggeds as it is for those that fly.

HOW TO PAD YOUR HOME WITH LOVE

Many parents spend much time, effort, and money on getting the house ready for the arrival of a child. That is good. Now, how about investing at least as much effort, time, and money in preparing yourselves *emotionally, mentally, and spiritually*? A loving family and a home filled with harmony and respect are the best protection against the bruises, emotional as well as physical, that are part of childhood.

Let's begin with the grownups. Have you worked out your differences with your mate, or with other adults living in your home? Is your relationship harmonious? If your answer is no, it is time to do something about it. The effort you make now will pay handsome dividends in terms of your bonding with your child.

IMPROVING YOUR RELATIONSHIPS

Open, honest communication is the basic building block for harmonious connecting. Both negative and positive feelings need to be expressed verbally, in a respectful manner. This can be accomplished by means of a method called *feeling talk*, which teaches us to take responsibility for our emotions. We do that by stating our sentiment in terms of '*I*', as in myself, rather than you.

VERBALIZING FEELINGS APPROPRIATELY

A common assumption is that those who are close to us know what we are thinking. Fortunately for most of us, that is not the case. So, when people do something for you that makes you happy, tell them that. It's a way of returning the favor. Tell your spouse and your children that you love them. They need to hear it; and don't forget to say *thank you*. We go to great lengths teaching our offspring to say *please*. How often do you show them how to give thanks by thanking them? Showing your appreciation is a way of expressing unconditional love. It can give a warm feeling to both the donor and the receiver.

Expressing Positive Feelings

1. Breathing slowly and deeply, become still.
2. Become aware of a positive feeling, such as thankfulness, love, or joy.
3. Write down the feeling in your journal, starting with *I am . . . (e. g.,* grateful, happy, etc.).
4. Speak to the person toward whom you have that feeling saying, e. g., *I thank you for . . .* , or *I am happy that . . .* (Fill in the blanks).
5. Write down your feelings and perceptions.

Many people find it difficult to verbalize negative feelings, or to express them in a caring way. The emotions may be overpowering, making it difficult for us to speak rationally. Most of us did not find the *feeling talk* in the cradle. We tend to revert to childhood ways of communicating when we feel pressured.

The following two exercises will show you how to verbalize negative feelings in a respectful manner.

Expressing Negative Feelings

1. Breathing slowly and deeply, become quiet.
2. Become aware of a negative feeling, such as anger, sadness, emotional pain, guilt, shame, fear, frustration. You may feel more than one emotion at a time.
3. Write your feeling(s) down.

Express your emotion to the person toward whom you feel negative, using the *feeling talk*, described below.

Feeling Talk

Prepare for the meeting by practicing out loud, so that you can hear yourself, ahead of actually doing it. This will give you more control over the way in which you express yourself. You can role play with another person, enlist your stuffed animals (I hope that you have at least one, for your inner child!), or do it with an imaginary friend.

Next, approach the individual to whom you wish to verbalize your feelings. You might say, *I have something I'd like to discuss with you. Do you have a few minutes?* Schedule a time that is convenient for both of you. Make sure that there is privacy for both of you. Bring up only one topic at a time, to prevent confusion.

Just before the meeting, take several deep breaths to help you relax. If possible, both of you should be at the same eye level. Maintain eye contact. When you are ready to begin, state your case in the following sequence.

1. *I am* . . . (State the feeling, e.g., hurt, angry, sad, frustrated, afraid, etc.).
2. *Because* . . . (Briefly state the reason).
3. *I wish you would* . . . (Say what you want your listener to do differently).
4. Write down your feelings, thoughts, and inspirations.

Now release and let go of any leftover negative feelings, by yourself, with *I am releasing and letting go of* . . . (Plug in your feelings, one at a time).

Since we cannot read each other's mind, we must rely on the spoken word. To that end, state *how* you feel, *why* you feel that way, and *what* you want. We say *I* rather than *you* to avoid finger-pointing. We are responsible for our own feelings. Blaming only serves to escalate arguments. The reasons given for your feelings are best kept brief and to the point, lest you lose the attention of your audience. What you want from your listener, however, needs to be explained in detail, in a positive fashion. The following example will illustrate how it's done.

Mary confronts husband Peter, who just walked in, "I'm really angry because you're late. I wish you would remember to come home on time so I can get to my class."

Notice that Mary stays with one issue, which she explains briefly. She avoids "always" and "never", loaded words that, like blaming, serve no purpose other than to escalate an argument. By resisting the temptation to tell him what he should have done, Mary shows that she does not expect Peter to be able to change the past. She explains explicitly what she wants from Peter, not expecting him to read her mind.

Peter now has a choice. He can apologize, or give Mary a reason for being late. He can also verbalize his own feelings. First, however, he needs to let Mary know that he hears her. This validates her feelings, and makes it more likely that she will hear him.

Peter tells Mary "I understand how you feel." He adds "I apologize for being late. There was an accident on my way home and I couldn't get through. I feel hurt that you made the assumption that I would forget."

Mary accepts his apology and his explanation by saying "I understand, that must have been frustrating. I forgive you." She adds "I apologize for jumping to conclusions." Peter says "I forgive you too!" They hug and feel good about each other again.

End of discussion. There was no energy wasted on unproductive arguing. Both got their feelings out, they heard each other, and both validated each other. Their self-esteem remains intact. Their respect for each other has probably grown. Love can flourish under these conditions.

COMMUNICATION

Respect and open communication are essential components of unconditional love. When they are present in the family, love thrives. When you engage in them with your spouse, your offspring will copy you. These attributes are more important than any material thing you might give them. When you communicate acceptance and love to your children consistently without conditions, when you tell them that you love them, every day, and when you give them a hug at least once a day, they will respect, love and trust you.

Please turn the page for a recipe for a loving relationship with your spouse.

RECIPE FOR A LOVING RELATIONSHIP WITH YOUR SPOUSE

Start with a healthy dose of respect,

Add give-and-take,

Stir in lots of open communication,

Sprinkle with understanding,

Add a big pinch of accepting each other's differences,

Blend with equality, and

Say "I love you" often . . . and mean it!

Take this mixture daily,

And love and trust will grow from it

Every day.

Sweeten it with sex

And enjoy your loving relationship!

COMMUNICATION AND DIVORCED PARENTS

Communication between the parents continues to be important when you separate or divorce. Responsible fathers and mothers make sure that communication channels stay open between them; for there is still much to discuss for the continuing welfare of their children. The feeling talk is the ideal tool. Be sure to communicate with each other directly. When you talk to one another through your offspring, it places a burden on them that they are not prepared to handle. Children become confused and torn in their loyalties when their parents speak disrespectfully about each other. They need to be able to continue loving both mother and father without guilt. When this is not the case, they may develop serious emotional and physical problems.

COMMUNICATION FOR STEP-PARENTS AND STEP-CHILDREN

Blending two families takes years. Start with cultivating the soil before you plant the seed, then water and fertilize *gently*. In other words, let the youngsters look you over before you move into the home, give them a chance to get to know you, and be low-key in your approach. Focus on being a friend and playmate. You will need to earn their trust. Be patient. Do not insist on being called Mom or Dad. These terms are reserved for the biological parents. Let the children address you by your first name.

If you have not been a member of the family from the youngster's early childhood, it is best to refrain from disciplining, even after you move in. Let the biological parent do that. Do express your feelings, non-judgmentally, with the feeling talk that I described earlier. Be sure to work out a strategy with your spouse or partner in order to arrive at a consensus before disciplining, to prevent confusion for everyone. You will save yourself and the family tons of tension by practicing an ounce or two of prevention this way.

PREPARING FOR BABY'S ARRIVAL

Once the home is set up and you have developed a warm, loving relationship with each other, you may feel ready to think about starting a family. Be sure to prepare yourselves for this event as carefully as you would for any other career.

Preparation for your baby's arrival starts long before conception. You have the honor to participate with the Creator in the creation of a new human being. Loving parents work on clearing negativity out of their hearts, minds, emotions, and bodies before they even attempt getting pregnant. They balance themselves physically, emotionally, and spiritually. Thus they prepare the soil for the planting of the human seed.

Cleansing and balancing yourself can be accomplished in several ways. Exercise tones your body and your mind and strengthens your muscles. Taking some good sweats in a sauna assists your body in releasing toxins and negatives that have piled up, clearing your mind and emotions in the process. Check with your physician first, however, if you cannot tolerate heat or have other health problems. Meditation enables you to open your heart and tap into your subconscious mind, your inner healer. Most spiritual and religious traditions include meditation in some form. Choose one to which you can relate. Ancient Native American ceremonies for releasing negativity from the heart, body, mind, and spirit are spiritual and meaningful. They are held in most parts of the United States and many are open to non-natives.

If you need instruction in any of the many methods for cleansing and balancing yourself, or want more information, check holistic journals and directories, as well as the Yellow Pages, or call colleges and libraries for classes available in your community. For Native American approaches, contact the offices of tribes, nations, or reservations in your area, to ensure that you are directed to qualified practitioners trained in the authentic ways.

You may already be aware of the damaging effects that alcohol, nicotine, and other drugs have on the fetus. Make sure that *both* of you get them out of your system and avoid them for the sake of the child, as well as yourselves. Negative feelings, like anger, hurt, sadness, fear, frustration, guilt, and shame, unresolved and still present in your bodies prior to and during conception, can affect the baby as much as any of these harmful substances. While cleansing, focus on *releasing* negative thoughts and emotions as described in Chapter 3.

Let's do another exercise for letting go of toxic feelings.

Releasing and Letting Go of Negative Feelings

1. Quiet yourself by focusing on your breathing.
2. Picture yourself surrounded with light.
3. Become aware of your anger, hurt, fear, guilt, or shame.
4. Closing your eyes, picture both hands of the Creator, cupped open.
5. See yourself dropping your negative feelings into His hands, one by one.
6. Fill the void left by this release with light.
7. Ask for guidance with your situation.
8. Give thanks.
9. Write down your feelings and thoughts.

Once body, mind, and emotions have been cleared, go into your heart or spirit, using meditation or prayer. You might ask the Creator, your higher power, angels, or guides, to assist you. How do you meditate? Let's check it out. This is an introduction. Further instruction in meditation is available in most communities.

Do the following exercise in a quiet place, and surround yourself with peaceful, harmonious music.

Introduction to Meditation

1. Become still by focusing on your breathing.
2. Take in deep rhythmic breaths.
3. With eyes closed, imagine or visualize a bright, beautiful light above you, in whatever color presents itself.
4. Gently draw this light all around yourself.
5. Go back to the source of the light and draw more of the light into yourself.
6. Notice how that feels. Focus your inner eye on the light for a few minutes.

Open your eyes and write down what you experienced.

When your minds, bodies and souls have been cleansed, you are you ready for attempting conception. The feelings of balance and inner peace derived from the purification and the knowledge that you have given something precious to your future child, will help you relax as you give the Creator the clear message, "We are ready to welcome, with love, a child into our midst."

SIX

A Child Is Born:
Conception, Birth and Infancy

I was just there,
Amidst light and joy!
Where am I now?
My body's so small,
I feel quite lost.
Hold me,
Hold me close,
Oh keep me safe!

Now that you have prepared yourselves and your home with love, you are ready to invite the soul of your child into the body which you are going to provide. Conception is the next step.

EMOTIONAL AND SPIRITUAL ASPECTS OF CONCEPTION

When couples love each other unconditionally, their sexual relationship becomes deeply spiritual and joyful. Sex makes possible an intimacy that is at once physical, emotional, mental, and spiritual. When love is conditional however, it is difficult to develop the *trust* that is a prerequisite for this closeness. The relationship tends to become more and more strained, making conception difficult.

While people long for intimacy, many men and women have a deep fear of being both physically and emotionally intimate with their partner. This type of closeness engenders a letting go of self, a willingness to blend energies on all levels. Is it any wonder that it scares so many? Yet like so many fears, this one is quite unfounded. Actually, when both partners accept themselves and each other without judgment or conditions, the intimacy develops naturally, on all levels; and the relationship becomes more joyful.

MAKING YOUR RELATIONSHIP MORE JOYFUL

Felicia and George very much wanted to have a baby. They felt that their lives were somehow incomplete without a child. Every time they made love, they focused on conception, and were bitterly disappointed when nothing happened. They put so much pressure on themselves and each other that they quite forgot to enjoy the process of getting there. The therapist, whom they eventually consulted, reminded them that pregnancy is not something that they can make happen. Rather than concentrating on the end result, they learned to pay attention to each other, while they turned their goal over to the Creator. They rediscovered their joy in each other and their relationship grew stronger. Much to their surprise, they soon became pregnant.

To bring more joy into your lovemaking, start with relaxing. Become more playful, have fun. If you have forgotten how, review the section on playfulness in Chapter 4. Communication is as important here as in the other areas of your relationship. Tell your partner how you like to be touched.

Sex is a right-brained activity. If the constant chatter of the left brain distracts you from abandoning yourself to emotional and physical closeness with your partner, you might try another right-brain event, such as music, to get you on course.

MUSIC HELPS SHIFT YOUR FOCUS.

The key is to choose music that you both like. Plan your selection *together*, well before you make love. Make sure that it plays without interruption for as long as you need it. Radio is not a good idea. There are interruptions from commercials, and you have no control over the selections. Television is a most distracting medium. How can you tune in to pleasing yourself and your partner, when you have one ear and an eye on the telly?

What do you do with the music? Once all your preparations are done, you turn the stereo on, *before* you start making love. It helps you to get in the mood for the next step, foreplay.

FOREPLAY BEGINS LONG BEFORE THE TRYST

Foreplay starts with being loving, and with doing nice things for your beloved. Tell and show each other that you want to be together and that you love one another. Give him a rose of his favorite color, send her an unexpected treat. Little love notes are usually appreciated. Bring out the candles; let the recorder answer your phone. If possible, take a romantic, relaxing bath together.

ABANDONING YOURSELF TO GOOD FEELINGS

Give your left brain a rest. Pay attention to the messages that all your senses are giving you. Listen to your body. Let it lead you in pleasuring each other. Communicate, let your beloved know what you like. Ask for more. Lovingly tell each other what does not feel comfortable, and support one another in working it out. This is unconditional loving at its best.

SEXUAL DIFFICULTIES

There are wonderful ways to enhance your sexual relationship. You will find them described in some of the books that I have listed for you in the bibliography section at the end of this book. If you have been abused as a child, or have another unresolved issue that keeps getting in the way, contact a professional, such as a family therapist, to help you work it through. If the problem is physical, see a gynecologist or urologist.

Chiropractors make adjustments to your spine that improves musculoskeletal functioning. Healthful nutrition, appropriate supplements, exercise, herbs, acupuncture, and homeopathic remedies, may improve sexual functioning as well.

Do feelings of embarrassment prevent you from getting help? Release them, let them go as I have taught you. Are you really willing to sacrifice a satisfying sexual relationship for something as useless as shame? I assure you that you are not the first to encounter sexual difficulties. It is quite normal to experience a decrease in libido during stress, illness, losses, depression, and anxiety. Some medications, as well as alcohol, nicotine, and other drugs can have the same effect.

CONCEPTION

Once your child has been conceived, you, Mom, nurture it lovingly within your body, emotionally, as well as physically. Dad, your role is to hold and support your wife with love, to enable her to carry out this task. There will be times that you will have to place your needs behind those of mother and child. *You can do it, guys!* Once you have cleansed yourself of negative energies, once you love unconditionally, you are able to do this with compassion and understanding.

SUPPORT FOR DAD

Though the importance of fathering has come to be acknowledged more fully, the support system for our dads is still incomplete. Today many men are willing to take their place in making their contribution to child-raising. They need and deserve emotional and spiritual nurturing as much as mothers do. Who is in a better position to provide this than those who have gone through it themselves? Parents, extended family, in-laws, friends, neighbors, can all be there for the husbands and fathers.

If family and friends are not available, the community needs to step in to provide this cushion. How about volunteer programs, consisting of experienced moms and dads who are willing to serve as a caring safety net for both fathers and mothers? Such assistance greatly reduces the fears and stress of those new to parenting. It also removes the need for ineffective and harmful substitutes, such as alcohol, drug, child, and spouse abuse.

For the parenting assistants, the return is precious. They know that they are giving something that is priceless, their unconditional love. And they soon learn that they and their skills are still needed, even though their own children might be grown. For humanity, this recycling of mothering and fathering expertise is invaluable. No more feelings of being useless and unwanted among the older population; reduced stress and increased confidence among young parents; and children who float along in a pink bubble of love! What a win/win situation!

PREPARING FOR LABOR AND DELIVERY

Pregnancy is a time for parents to dream about their baby and think about what to call it. Ask, in prayer or meditation, for the most suitable name for this soul. Visualize an easy labor and delivery, and plan the infant's environment in the home.

If possible, both parents need to be involved in the preparation for the infant's arrival. Historically, too many of these tasks have been laid upon women. Mother is putting all her energy into growing this new human being within her. Father's input is important, not only to assist her, but also for his male perception and energy.

Together, male and female form the body of the baby. Both genders have much to contribute to the further development of the little one. Children thrive basking in the love of mother *and* father. Who would want to deprive them of that?

Talk to the baby in the womb, put your arms around it, and stroke it. Sing to it, play music to it. It can hear the sounds you make, the music in your home. It can also hear arguments, put downs, and fights. What do you want your child to hear?

THE ABSENTEE FATHER

If the father of your child is not available, find someone among your family or friends who is qualified to be a substitute father figure to your child. This needs to be someone whom you trust, perhaps a grandfather, an uncle, or a friend. He need not live with you. If he can be available to be an appropriate male role model for your son or daughter from time to time, you and your child will benefit greatly.

EMOTIONAL AND SPIRITUAL NEEDS DURING LABOR AND DELIVERY

Health professionals have done much to make labor and delivery more pleasant for mother, father and child. However, birthing is still totally consuming to the women going through it. Mothers, you open yourself up physically, emotionally, and spiritually. Thus, you need to be surrounded with love, positive feelings, and harmony. Ground yourself in Grandmother Earth; notice that you are supported by her who knows everything about giving birth.

Fathers, you will, of course, do everything in your power to be present for and supportive to your wife or partner during this blessed event. Your loving male energy is much needed to assure a smooth entry for this soul into our world, and to assist mom in her heroic task of giving birth.

The community can participate by encouraging fathers to take time off to be present at the birth of their children. Volunteer helpers from among those having gone through this before, can do much to ease the process for mom and dad.

SPECIAL NEEDS OF SINGLE MOTHERS

It is crucial that single moms decide who will be present during labor and birthing and immediately after it. If you do not have a good relationship with the father of your child, it is better that he not be there. Negative feelings between you will prove toxic to you and the child. Yes, men, your feelings are important, too. I ask you, nevertheless, to practice unconditional love for your child and its mother by showing understanding for their situation.

THE EMOTIONAL NEEDS OF THE INFANT

Feeling loved, safe and secure are the first emotional needs. Being born is as taxing for the child, as the delivery is for mom and dad. The trip down the birth canal is much like a roller coaster ride. It is most frightening for such a wee person. Assuring emotional security for the newborn will help it feel safe, as well as wanted.

The first task of the infant is to survive and grow. The responsibility of all those involved with it is to make that possible. Throughout the first year of life, unconditional love and acceptance continue to be as important as food and shelter. In order to be able to develop, babies *need* to be loved. Emotional closeness, holding, and touching, all will permit the child to thrive. Talk to the baby. Let it know that you love it. Sing to it, play together, and stimulate its senses and intellect with colors and age-appropriate toys.

PROVIDING SECURITY FOR YOUR CHILD

Babies are very sensitive to the emotions of the people around them, especially to those of their mothers. If you feel frightened, your little one feels that way too. So, if you want the baby to feel safe, it is important to feel secure yourself. Release and let go of fears and ask the Creator to guide you. Keep balancing yourself physically, mentally, emotionally, and spiritually, using any of the methods that I described earlier.

Accept the child as it is, even if it did not come out as you expected it to be. Demonstrate your love by comfortably enclosing your little one in your arms, smiling, and uttering soothing sounds to it. Tell it that you love it. At the soul level, your child will understand and remember every word! When you start doing this right after birth, it will help you and the baby bond with each other. If you are not experienced in holding babies, go to the following exercise. Do it together with your mate if possible.

Helping the Infant Feel Secure

1. Find a doll or stuffed animal for practicing.
2. Cradle it in your arms, pretending that it is a child.
3. Find a way of holding it comfortably, close to you but not too tightly.
4. Relax; trust yourself to be able to do it.
5. Now pick up your baby and hold it securely in your arms, just as you held the doll, for as long as you wish
6. Place the child in a safe place.
7. Write down your feelings and insights.

INFANTS UNDERSTAND MORE THAN YOU THINK,

From birth, babies react to sounds, to changes in temperature and their environment. Soon, they look around and observe those around them. It does not take long for them to internalize what they see. Much sooner than most adults think, they begin to imitate us. What do you want them to pick up from you? Let's do another exercise. Do this one as a couple, if possible.

Tuning In To Your Baby

1. Get on the floor on a cushion or blanket, with the child.
2. Lay the baby down, face up; making sure it is safely supported.
3. Get in a comfortable position on the floor.
4. Observe the little one for at least 15 minutes.
5. Notice behaviors, facial expressions and sounds.
6. Touch the infant gently, observe the reaction.
7. Notice what happens when you touch the hands.
8. Pick up the child, cradle it in your arms, and talk to it.
9. Put the baby in a safe place, and write down your reactions and feelings.

Do this as often as possible. It is a great bonding exercise.

HOW TO EASE THE TRANSITION OF YOUR NEWBORN INTO EARTH SPACE

By preparing yourselves and your home with unconditional love for your baby, you are assuring a smooth path of entry for it. Can you imagine what life will be like for this child, made thus welcome? With total acceptance, respect, and nurturing without judgment or condition, from conception on, this little one will be able to flower and grow without anything holding it back.

SEVEN

Early Childhood:
Exploring and Absorbing

I want to taste this world,
To touch and smell it!
I want to be like you
And do the things you do!
So I say NO!
Just like you!
I need you to
Love me,
As I am.

THE TERRIFIC TWO'S AND THREE'S

Much maligned as being "terrible", this is in fact a magical period for the child. After the first year of life, youngsters increasingly shift their focus to their environment. Everything excites their curiosity. Once they are mobile, there is no stopping them. With enthusiasm as boundless as their energy, they zoom around on all fours, or toddle on the brink of falling, drawn like a magnet to the very place you don't want them to be. Totally fearless, they do not know the meaning of the word "impossible." These tots are compulsive about investigating their world and stretching their boundaries, and they are *fast!* So, be sure to move potentially harmful objects out of their reach to prevent injury.

Little ones are quick to imitate our favorite exclamation of alarm, precipitated by their forays into imminent danger. The lusty *"NO!" of* a two-year-old might be the envy of any adult needing to learn that two-letter word! Though cute at first, it soon becomes utterly frustrating. Refrain from punishing, however, gentle reader. It's a time to rejoice instead.

The first step toward independence and decision-making, your toddler's *no* is as important as the first attempt at walking unaided. Each is a stepping stone toward defining identity. That is exactly what children need to accomplish in order to make a healthy transition into the next phase.

38

When toddlers are reined in too tightly, when they are denied the freedom to express themselves, their development is hampered.

A single mother, Alice had her hands full keeping up with three-year-old Billy, and her four month old daughter, Tanya. Since Tanya required much attention, Alice had less time to spend with Billy. She planted him in front of the television in order to keep him busy, but Billy became more and more demanding. When he threw temper tantrums to get her attention, Alice locked him in his room to "keep him out of trouble" while she was busy. Now Billy, already toilet trained, started to soil himself again. He reverted to baby talk and started to cling to his mother.

What happened? Barely out of baby shoes himself, Billy became more and more desperate. Feeling rejected, he also recognized that infant behaviors got his mother's attention. He engaged in these behaviors to get what he needed. This situation, if it were to go on unabated, could cause Billy harm that might trail him into adulthood. I have seen teens and young adults who would soil their pants when they felt emotionally neglected. The damages to self esteem, the emotional insecurity, due to rejection at this tender age, can have disastrous results in later life.

What might Alice do differently, in order to juggle the needs of both her children, as well as her own? Let's check it out. Since grownups are often preoccupied and thus may have trouble understanding what children say, we'll start with sharpening your listening skills.

Listening with Your Inner Ear

1. While the child is speaking to you, get on the same eye level.
2. Listen closely, maintaining eye contact.
3. Repeat out loud what you think you heard, in adult language, not baby talk.
4. If you did not understand, the youngster will correct you. Listen *patiently*.
5. Keep repeating what you hear until you get it right.
6. How did that feel? Write it down.

Now you are ready for the next step. You will need quiet time and solitude for the first part.

Helping Children Exercise Freedom of Choice (Part 1)

1. Become still, relax, and close your eyes.
2. Picture the child that you once were. Were you allowed to make choices?

What was that like? Write down your feelings about that situation.

Helping Children Exercise Freedom of Choice (Part 2)

1. Closing your eyes again, picture your child as a grown up.
2. See him or her engage in adult activities.
3. Imagine what expertise your son or daughter might need in that situation. Is making decisions part of that?
4. Come back into the present and visualize yourself supporting your little one in learning, *now*, some of the skills needed in the future.
5. Make a plan for putting your ideas into practice.
6. Write down your plan, and your feelings regarding it.

CHOICES, CHOICES: THE FABULOUS FOUR'S AND FIVE'S

Four and five-year-olds are increasingly independent. Ready to venture further into the world outside the home, they like to roam outdoors and engage in active play with friends. They need playmates. Yet, with an imagination that is boundless, pre-schoolers will readily invent buddies if they do not have any. This ability to fantasize, coupled with blossoming creativity, quite naturally attracts them to engage in arts and crafts.

Children in this age group are emphatic about making their own decisions. On the other hand, it can be overwhelming for them to have too many choices. The answer is to give them only two options to choose from. This makes it easier to make a selection. A good place to start is to let them pick out the clothes which they are going to wear, one day at a time. Initially, give them only two outfits to choose from. Honor their selection. Later on, you can teach how to coordinate clothing if the pieces don't match. Make it fun for you and them. This is an opportunity for both of you to bond! Catch yourself when you are tempted to be controlling.

Write down your feelings in your journal.

THE PERILS OF EARLY CHILDHOOD

When I see the amount of stress to which little children are exposed, I wonder how any of them survive, let alone thrive.

Let's take a look at some of these perils. Having endured the difficult roller coaster ride through the birth canal and successfully drawn his first breath, little Johnny must almost immediately face a painful challenge: circumcision. Then, for both genders, respiratory and ear infections give way to gastrointestinal disorders, to be succeeded by contagious childhood diseases, with one or another happening about every four to six weeks. Every new tooth announces its arrival with excruciating pain, usually accompanied by tummy aches, diarrhea or constipation, nasal congestion, and/or diaper rash. Then there are the bumps, bruises, and fractures associated with falling and being dropped. Do you still wonder why babies get irritable and go through spells of crying?

Another hazard, a more recent arrival, is equally harmful to the little ones. Parents are pushing children to succeed earlier in life than ever before in our culture. This may be due to the fear that their offspring might not succeed in life, or that they might not get into those prestigious schools. The pressure to accomplish more than they are developmentally able to do causes children much anxiety.

Sucking her thumb, one-year-old Maggie is perched in front of the television, more or less watching a video that features the alphabet. Eighteen-month old Bobby is fingering puzzle pieces that are covered with numbers, while his mother is telling him their names. Betsy is anxiously running around a table covered with books and toys that are beyond her two-year-old ability to comprehend.

The pressure to get toilet trained has been replaced by the push to hurry up and learn the alphabet and numbers before age two. Is it surprising that the incidence of hyperactive (read obsessive/compulsive) behavior among small children is on the increase? We are raising a generation of youngsters that are destined to become driven to compete and excel! How can these boys and girls develop their imaginations and dream their dreams, when every minute of the day is programmed with spoon-fed information?! Does that even make sense in this computer age? Remember, computers are very good with numbers and spelling, but they have no imagination whatsoever!

MENTAL AND EMOTIONAL NEEDS IN EARLY CHILDHOOD

The emotional needs of children going through this stage of growth include *security, stability, lots of love and I love you's, and plenty of hugging*. It is scary to grow up in an insecure world. Telling them that you love them, holding them, and hugging them, all help the little ones feel wanted. A peaceful environment that is at least somewhat predictable gives them a sense of safety. When you read a story to youngsters in this age group, they want no deviation from the way it was told before. If you forget, they will remind you repeatedly how it goes. And their memories are uncanny. They will repeat the tale word for word, quite easily.

When boys and girls are healthy, their energy is boundless. Their curiosity extends to everything. They learn effortlessly and seem to soak up information like a sponge.

My granddaughter was barely two years old, when the mail man came to the door one day with a big package that was covered completely with transparent tape. I set it aside. Pretty soon, I noticed that the little girl had become very quiet. I checked to see what she was doing, and there she was, poking away at the tape with her little fingers, looking for an opening to peel it off the package! I was just thinking "there's no way she can do that", when she found it. In no time at all, she was merrily yanking the tape off the box. Her curiosity was aroused, there was no stopping her. She tackled the problem and solved it, all by herself.

It is up to us to stimulate the imagination of youngsters, rather than suppressing it; and to foster their can-do attitude, rather than reining it in. The first few years of life are crucial for children. Voraciously, they absorb, process, and store information. Give them simple toys that foster imagination. Let them draw and paint and try out their problem solving skills.

Encourage them to dance and sing, and tell you stories. Pre-schoolers are keen observers. It is delightful to have one of them present during a family session. At this age, children see things realistically and talk about them with sincerity and candor.

The possibilities are endless. When we ignore these opportunities, we hurt not only our offspring. We also harm ourselves and our society. When we nurture their imagination and encourage their hunger for learning, we can help youngsters expand their intelligence and increase their self esteem. Imagine the talents that will flower once we manage to do this! Picture the contributions that these children will make as adults.

The first few years of life are the most impressionable in all of childhood. What adults do and say is accepted without question. Every word, good or bad, becomes engraved upon the mind of a child. Experiences at this age have an incredible impact on the entire belief system of the individual. Children who are abused, or mistreated, may come to believe that the world is a bad place and that grownups are not to be trusted. Those who are raised with love and understanding, on the other hand, will likely develop into compassionate adults.

So, choose your words and actions with great care. When your little one is hurt, hug it and console it as soon as you possibly can. While this cannot erase the pain from the child's memory, it does much to soften it.

BED-TIME SCENARIOS

Megan, normally an adorable child, became defiant at bed time. She loved to be with Mom and Dad, especially since they were gone all day. When it was time to go to bed, she would cling to them and put up such a fuss that they would hold and rock her for two hours, until she finally fell asleep. By that time their evening was gone and they would both be exhausted.

This scenario is repeated every evening, in countless homes across our land. The fact is that many youngsters resist going to bed during times of transition, such as moving from crib to bed, when another baby is on the way or has arrived, and during any stress experienced by them or the family. Always in need of stability, they react to any change, even the beneficial kind, with anxiety that interferes with sleep. Does this ring a bell?

Megan's parents found out that there were several things that they could do to get relief. They created a *peaceful, harmonious* atmosphere in their home by avoiding arguments, loud music, overly stimulating play or exercise, and upsetting television programs, especially before bed time. They talked over their problems outside the reach of Megan's ears. They asked the baby sitter to stay a little longer, so that they could take a walk together to balance themselves before they came home. And they gave Megan the evening meal at least an hour before bed time, avoiding sweets that would make her more wakeful.

When Megan seemed fearful, they encouraged her to talk about her fears of being alone, of the dark, and any other feelings that keep her awake. When she could not do that, they asked her to draw a picture of the problem. When it was finished, they asked her to explain the action in the drawing. They let her do the talking and listened carefully. Pictures, like dreams, can tell us symbolically what youngsters are feeling. Megan drew a little girl that was being chased by a monster, indicating fears of getting hurt, or feelings about having been harmed in some way. Megan's Dad said, "I guess maybe you are scared. Let's talk about it." Her Mom reassured her, "We are here with you. Let us together figure out a way to keep you safe and to take care of this". They held her and rocked her, and soon she was fast asleep. Gradually bed time became an event that everyone looked forward to, including Megan.

If your child refuses to talk, avoid pushing. Instead, ask for more drawings. Boys and girls usually like to talk about their art work. So be patient. Never, criticize their work, lest you inhibit that creative form of expression.

Guide children to come down slowly from the events of the day. A good way to do that, is to tell or read them a bed time story *that is not upsetting*. Have the child get comfortably settled in bed before you start. Sit close by. Keep the length of time to about ten to fifteen minutes. End with a brief tucking-in ceremony, a hug, and *I love you*. That is an opportunity to do some bonding. If at all possible, repeat the process on a daily basis. Begin it with the firm expectation that the youngster will stay in bed and go to sleep, lest the little rascal pick up on your wavering and use it to manipulate you.

THE IMPORTANCE OF PLAY

Play is indispensable during all of childhood, and especially at this time. To children, play is what work is to adults, and much more. It is their occupation, their education, their socialization, and their recreation. When you take play time and play things away, you retard their emotional growth and their intellectual and creative development!

To help youngsters get the most out of their childhood, play with them, sing and dance with them, teach them songs of childhood, and read them stories. Avoid telling them what to play. At best, make suggestions, like *how about singing a song*, or *wouldn't it be fun to draw a picture?* Let them choose. This encourages creativity and sharpens their decision-making skills. Let's see how it is done.

Sharing Playtime with Children

1. Get on the same eye level with the little one. Sit on the floor, if that is where the action is, close by, but not too close.
2. Watch from the sidelines while the youngster plays.
3. Slowly ease in and join in the game, letting the child guide you.
4. Listen and try to understand what he or she is saying.
5. Respond as needed, but refrain from taking over.
6. If you are not invited to join the play, don't take it personally. Instead, play along on the sidelines.
7. Suggest an activity like singing, but limit yourself to one.
8. The attention span of small children is short. When they tire, it is time to stop, or to do something else.

When play time is over, write down your feelings and insights.

If you find it difficult to do this exercise, or you want to learn more about playing with your children, you might want to consult a play therapist.

When you play with your offspring, sing with them, or read to them, you give them something which they require in order to thrive: emotional *nurturing*. When children do not receive that support, they will demand attention with negative behaviors. Those who are nurtured in a dependable, sustained way are much less demanding.

SETTING LIMITS AND BOUNDARIES

Figuring out how to set limits can be quite challenging at this stage of childhood. Needing to explore their surroundings in order to grow mentally and emotionally, on one hand, youngsters may get hurt, on the other, since they know no fear. By all means, make sure that they don't injure themselves seriously, but avoid overprotection, which would stunt their emotional growth.

Fortunately, there is an alternative. Teach children to explore *safely*, by showing them how to do it. When my older daughter, then six-months old, insisted on going up and down stairs even before she could walk, I got on my hands and knees and showed her how to crawl both up and down, all the while explaining how it's done. When I was satisfied that she knew how, I let her do it by herself. From then on, she negotiated the stairs successfully, neither falling nor hurting herself.

Even little ones will tell us when we are holding them back, by word, or by action. They may say, "I can do it!", or "let me, let me!", or they may get irritable or cranky. Listening is everything with children. By observing them and listening with *love and patience*, you will soon know what they are trying to say.

Always explain first what you are about to do, in language which kids can understand. Be patient! You are speaking to a little one who may not comprehend your words. Use *show and tell* and educate *by example*. Teach your child respect by being respectful yourself. You are being observed and imitated. When we treat children with consideration, even when disciplining, they learn to be considerate toward us.

As their range expands, boys and girls alike take more risks. Increasingly, they want to spend more time with play mates and less with Mom and Dad. This is normal. Support your child lovingly in these endeavors. Set limits without being too restrictive. Listen to your child. Develop the habit to get to know friends and their families. Let your youngster make age-appropriate choices. This will help him/her learn to make decisions.

Limit-setting applies to buying toys as well. Explain with love that your child cannot have everything that they see advertised. Get toys that encourage and develop imagination, rather than those that come completely pre-programmed. My children loved to play with the clothes pins and pots and pans that they saw me use. I can report that their imagination has flourished, and they have become very creative adults.

DISCIPLINING CHILDREN IN THE EARLY YEARS

Discipline at this age needs to be gentle. Explain rather than criticize, keep your voice at a normal pitch, and place yourself physically at the same level as the child. Look straight into his/her eyes and speak with love, not anger. Your little one will hear you better that way.

Avoid spanking. Hitting youngsters teaches them only one thing: that it is permissible to hurt people. Is that the message you want to give them? Listen to your own words. Make sure that they are positive and nurturing. Build self esteem, do not tear it down. Remember, it all registers in the mind of the child.

State your requests in positive terms. It is more effective to say, 'put your feet on the floor please" than "don't put your feet on the couch!" In the latter statement, your child hears only *put your feet on the couch!* No wonder those little feet don't go down to the floor! Let's do another exercise.

Listening To Yourself

1. Set up a tape recorder with a recording tape that runs for at least 45 minutes on one side.
2. Set the recorder on *record*, before you start interacting with the children.
3. Talk as you normally do. Keep the tape running until it stops.
4. When the time is up, listen to the tape.
5. How do you sound? What did you learn about yourself? Write it down, and add your feelings.

DISCIPLINING WITH LOVE

Time Out

One of the most effective ways to discipline at this age is *time out*. Some words of caution, however.

- To be effective, time out needs to be carried out with love, as a *learning experience*, rather than a jail sentence. Avoid overusing it.
- The youngster needs to be old enough to understand what is going on.
- The attention span of a little one is very short. Time out, therefore, should last no longer than *one or two minutes*.
- It should take place in the same room where you are, not in the child's room.
- To teach by example, sit down in a chair as well. Do nothing and refrain from looking at the child.

When you are ready to begin time out, have the youngster sit on a chair. Set a timer. Avoid stimuli, such as TV, radio, or visits from friends. Stick with the prearranged amount of time, lest you sacrifice trust. When the timer rings, time is up. Before rising from your chair, face the child and discuss the problem that led to time out, speaking in a normal voice. Be open to questions. Then give the youngster a hug and say *"I love you"*.

Now let's try it out ~ on you!

Time Out: For Grownups!

1. Set a timer for 15 minutes.
2. Switch off television and radio.
3. Quietly sit in a chair.
4. Refrain from answering the telephone or the door.
5. Do nothing.
6. Time is up when the timer rings.

How did you feel about being in time out for 15 minutes? Write it down.

If you managed to sit still for the full fifteen minutes, you did well. This is difficult for an adult to do. What do you think it is like for a child?

The Feeling Talk

One of the most effective ways to communicate, feeling talk, which I have explained in Chapter 5, works very well with this age group. Looking straight into the youngster's eyes, state your feeling one at a time, give a brief reason, and explain what you want. Be sure to use simple language and short sentences. Here's an example. *I'm mad because you don't come when I call you. I want you to come right away when I call.* Notice that there is no blaming here, and no beating around the bush. What gets the child's attention is talk that is direct, to the point, and compassionate. Keeping the level of your voice just above a whisper rather than raising it will encourage your child to listen more closely.

Consequences

Another way to discipline is by means of consequences. To illustrate, let's go to the animal world, to the winged ones, to see how they handle these situations.

Birds teach their young to fly with much patience and nurturing. When one of the little ones misses on take-off from the nest and rolls to the ground, the parents encourage it to fly back to the nest, all by itself. In their wisdom, they know that this baby would surely perish if it did not learn early to rely on itself.

Please note that I am **not** suggesting that you let your children roll on the ground and have them pick themselves up.

Of course, *consequences need to be age-appropriate.* Make sure that they are in the realm of *safety for the child.* Before you consider letting your youngster experience the results of his or her error, make sure that the situation is **not** life threatening, and that it will **not** cause physical, mental, or emotional harm. Only you can be the judge regarding the appropriateness of this approach for you and the child. If you are uncertain as to how to use it, consult a child therapist first.

Mistakes are learning experiences. Rather than scolding or blaming children for committing errors like spilling milk, encourage them to figure out what went wrong, and then ask "let's see what you can learn from this." Think back to your childhood. Did you learn from your mistakes when you were shamed or blamed for them? As a matter of fact, would you be able to do that even now, as an adult?

THE FINE ART OF PRAISING

Loving adults look for behaviors that they can applaud. Criticism has a tendency to breed more negative behaviors. Since youngsters love to be praised, they tend to engage in those behaviors which earn them your approval. Reinforce your verbal praise with a smile and a hug.

Avoid attacking the self worth of children when you discipline. A little one's self image is vulnerable and needs to be handled with care. Much like Humpty Dumpty, it is difficult to put it back together again, once it is broken. Praising, on the other hand, *builds* self esteem *for the youngster, as well as for you!* It is easy to give, and costs only time. The return on this investment, on the other hand, is priceless, for children, adults, and humanity!

OPPORTUNITY AND CHALLENGE

The foundation for a healthy, loving relationship with children is established during early childhood. Any efforts you make to treat them with *patience, respect, unconditional love, and understanding* will pay many dividends in the years to come. *Nurture* the little ones and listen to them. *Hug* them and *tell* them that you love them. *Encourage and support* them as they try their wings. Be *clear and consistent* in your expectations, but don't look for perfection. Be *gentle and non-judgmental* in your disciplining. Refuse to let fear or panic come between you. Release those feelings; let them go, before they turn into impatience and anger. Remember, angry words, hitting, and pushing around, stay with youngsters for a long, long time.

Observe the way in which animals rear their young. Have you ever seen a duck cross a street followed by thirteen ducklings, all lined up neatly, in tow? What does she do when one of the little ones lags behind? She waddles back to it and gently coaxes it to join the others. No screaming, no hitting! Have you ever observed trainers get Shamu, or any other animal performer, do anything for them with yelling or beating? They treat their charges with love, respect, and encouragement. Animal trainers communicate their expectations with consistency and clarity. Patiently, they teach and guide, reinforcing every correct action immediately with praise and rewards.

OUR CHILDREN DESERVE THE SAME UNCONDITIONAL LOVE, RESPECT, SUPPORT, AND NURTURING, FROM ALL OF US.

EIGHT

Middle Childhood: Expanding Horizons

I'm big, I can do anything!
I'm a tiger, see, SEE?
No wait; I'm a 'splorer, Columbus!
This is my ship, see?
I'm gonna find us a new world
For just you and me!
I want to learn,
Reach out, explore!
I want to dream my life!
Guide me and love me!
And, yes, I love you too.

THE MAGICAL MIDDLE YEARS

Middle childhood, extending from about six through nine years of age, is marked by tremendous mental and emotional expansion. Those youngsters, who have been allowed to develop with a healthy balance between security and independence in early childhood, appear to be driven to venture forth into the world and to try everything at least once. Full of energy and intensely curious, they ask questions endlessly and love to talk. Their imagination is magical. They make up fantastic stories and believe that *anything* is possible. They are fun to be with. They are also a challenge, and, with all that energy, quite exhausting to most adults.

MENTAL AND EMOTIONAL NEEDS IN THE MIDDLE YEARS

Having survived the perils of early childhood, boys and girls need support in their drive for independence, and loving guidance in their attempts to venture forth.

Seven-year old Bobby loved to race around the neighborhood on his new bike, paying scant attention to passing cars. His Mom, worried that he might get hurt, told him, "You are not allowed in the street anymore. Stay on the driveway." Bobby stayed there, but as soon as she went back into the house, he zoomed back into the road, oblivious to danger. When Mom confronted him about his behavior, he described, in great detail, a dragon that he had to chase away from the house.

This was a frustrating situation for Bobby's Mom. Realizing, however, that making up stories and taking risks come with this stage of development, she sat down with Bobby and listened to him. When he was done, she countered, "That must have been scary. You know, Bobby, I was scared, too. And I still am afraid, when I see you riding your bike right in front of a car." She went on to explain the potential consequences of this kind of behavior, in terms that he could understand. Then she said, "I want you to be more careful", explaining specifically how he could do that. In other words, she seized the opportunity to teach him the rules of the road for bicyclists, thereby making this a learning experience. She went for a bike ride with him on their quiet residential street until she was satisfied that he was implementing her teaching.

Let boys and girls try their wings within reason, while you are available as a coach and guide. Avoid reining them in too much. Provide plenty of opportunity for exercise to meet their need for motion and activity. When you participate in activities as a family, plan events that involve action to hold the youngsters' interest and let them work off steam. Encourage them to play outdoors where they can roam and burn up some of that abundant energy that they enjoy at this age.

Be sure to furnish plenty of intellectual stimulation and challenge. Board games and card games are favorites at these ages. At this stage, children are still delighted when their elders play a game with them. So, by all means, join them to promote family fun and togetherness. Keep things playful, however, avoid too much competition.

Keep the hugs and *I love you's* coming. As they reach the upper end of this age group, youngsters may ask you to do the hugging in privacy, however. Honor that request.

During pre-puberty both boys and girls are easily embarrassed as they become more and more concerned about what their peers think about them.

Continue to let children learn from their mistakes, as described in the previous chapter. Far from being failures, errors are valuable *learning experiences*. When we protect youngsters from their mistakes, or shame them for committing them, we attack their self worth. When we encourage them to take something positive away from those encounters, we actually help their self esteem grow. Let's see how that is done.

Mis-Takes: 'Missing' Something Can be turned into 'Taking away' New Learning

1. The next time your child makes a mistake, stop! And take a deep breath. Try not to get mad.
2. Instead, say to him/her, "Let's see what you can learn from this one".
3. Figure out together what went wrong. Listen to the youngster's input.
4. Ask, "How can you do it better next time"? It's worth waiting for the answer. It will be insightful.
5. Discuss the situation and provide appropriate guidance. Avoid preaching; children just tune it out.
6. Talk about your feelings and encourage the child to do the same.
7. Give praise for honesty and effort.
8. Write down your feelings and insights about this situation.

LET THERE BE PRAISE!

To reiterate what I said before, lauding youngsters for making an effort, and not only for doing things well, furthers self worth. This type of feedback, also referred to as *positive reinforcement*, is crucial to healthy development. Without praise, children wither emotionally. More important than criticism, praise lets them know that they are doing something correctly, that their behavior meets your expectations. Your applause actually encourages them to engage in that kind of behavior again. Isn't that what you want them to do? You get more of the behaviors that you want, and the youngsters get a lift for their self esteem. What a win/win situation! The only cost to you is a little time: time to observe the child's effort, time to utter some kind words. All of us, adults included, like to hear praise. The point is that we can all give it—and we may even get some back!

DISCOVERING TALENTS

Every boy and every girl has special gifts. One of the most crucial and gratifying tasks that everyone working with children has is to *identify* and *nurture* these talents. How is that done? Keep your eyes and ears tuned to youngsters in your care. When you discover a special ability, explore it gently, but do not push. Rather, let the mystery unfold. Yes, this requires patience on your part. But then, how many people do you know who were pressured, much to their detriment? Some even gave up on their gifts in frustration. You will know when the child is ready to do something with that ability. Then it is time to encourage and nurture that talent ~ and its owner ~ with love.

When children show an interest in sports, let them sample different ones prior to narrowing down the choices. Provide several options for them and guide them, but leave the final choice to them. Be supportive, cheer them on. Avoid putting pressure on them to excel, however. That would take the fun out of it, both for the youngster and for you. When my family and I lived in the Netherlands some years ago, my daughters played on a field hockey team. Much to my delight, the coach would address the team before each competition with "Remember, it's just a game! The sport is in the playing and functioning together as a team. If per chance you win the game, that's nice. And if you should lose, you will learn from it." The youngsters did as well as they were able to any way, but they had fun doing it. And they did not feel crushed when they lost.

LET'S TALK ABOUT CRITICISM

It is tempting, during this growth phase, to become more critical of children. What seemed cute in the four-year old can be blatantly irresponsible in the youngster with nine years under the belt. True, boys and girls in this age group require increasing amounts of responsibility in order to mature, but they still view the world from a child's limited perspective. Whenever your expectations are unrealistic, you place a burden on children that they are not ready to assume.

Dorothy, a young adult, was suffering from recurring anxiety and depression. Filled with an inner sense of failure, she was in a constant state of apprehension that made it difficult for her to find inner peace. She recalled that no matter how well she did in school, it was never good enough for her parents. When she brought home a report card that was brimming with A's, there was no pat on the back. Instead she was told, "If you can do this well, you can do better." As an adult she continued that kind of talk internally. She could not feel good about herself, no matter how many successes she had. As a result she became more depressed and avoided her friends. Unable to concentrate at work, she made mistakes and was in danger of losing her job.

I have found that the impact of high expectations during their youth often affects the recipients thereof, as well as their relationships with others, all the way into adulthood. It can take a great deal of therapy to work through that.

CRITIQUING CHILDREN WITH LOVE

In order to critique, rather than criticize, distinguish between the person and the behavior. In other words, rather than attacking the child verbally or physically, describe the conduct that you disapprove of. Be sure to let the individual know that you are making that distinction. Avoid being judgmental. Instead, critique behavior with love to encourage emotional growth and healthy self image. Give your feedback as soon as possible after the transgression, while it is still fresh in the mind of the child. Who can recall what happened a day or more ago?

Below is an example of critiquing behavior.

Giving Feedback

1. Review the *Feeling Talk* in Chapter 5.
2. Adapt the steps of the feeling talk to the issue at hand.
3. Express your feelings to the child, maintaining eye contact.
4. Explain what you want, with *I wish you would . . .*
5. Listen to the youngster's response.
6. Validate his/her feelings with *I understand how you feel.*
7. If necessary, add *but I still want you to . . .*
8. Make sure that you keep the *because*-statement brief and to the point.
9. Be explicit in your explanation of what you want, in *positive* terms.
10. How do you feel? Write it down.

For example, "I am angry because you just slapped your sister", is preferable to "you are a bad boy/girl." Explain in detail what behavior you are looking for, e. g., "I wish you would treat your sister with more respect." State what you *are* looking for, rather than what you don't want. When you say, "I don't want you to do that", youngsters hear, "want you to do that", and will do whatever it is that you don't want them to do. The good news is that when you use the feeling talk regularly with children, they soon imitate it. In this developmental phase, boys and girls still copy what you say and do.

Keep your expectations for any improvements low. *Be patient.* It takes time to make changes. Praise the efforts made, even if they seem small.

HOW DO YOU DISCIPLINE WITH LOVE AT THIS STAGE?

Discipline needs to be swift, brief, and to the point. Time out is still useful. Limit it to *two minutes or less,* however. Avoid lengthy grounding and drawn-out loss of privileges that lead to rebelliousness. A better way is total grounding for half a day, or, for a serious transgression such as lying, for a day. This entails loss of all privileges during the grounding, including TV, stereo, radio, calls in or out, and visits from friends. The youngster may be around you, however, may assist with household chores, and do homework. Nagging and treating him/her like a criminal shoot down self-esteem, and are thus counterproductive. Explaining your rationale in terms that the child can comprehend is much more effective, especially when done with love.

ABOUT LYING

In the vignette quoted earlier in this chapter, was Bobby lying when he told the dragon story? To find the answer to this question, keep his age in mind. Inventing incredible tales is part of this exciting phase. I am sure that the dragon was quite real to Bobby. The stories that boys and girls make up at this age indicate that their minds are expanding and that their imagination is growing.

So take pride in the youngster's story-telling ability. This is a talent that is to be nurtured and applauded. You may have a budding author there!

Children will fabricate when they are afraid, or don't know how to extricate themselves from a given situation. More often than not, they just don't understand what we want from them. Perhaps you have not stated your request in sufficient detail. This is a good time to sit down with your offspring, and find out what is going on, *listening carefully*. Express your feelings with the *feeling talk* and encourage them to do the same. Avoid asking why he or she lied.

Phrase your questions as statements, such as, *I wonder what happened*. Explain that it is not acceptable to lie. Present alternatives. Go over the options available, and demonstrate how to make choices. This is an opportunity for you to explain the difference between right and wrong and show, *by your example*, how to do it better.

PEER PRESSURE

During the latter part of middle childhood, around pre-puberty, boys and girls become more susceptible to peer-pressure. Very sensitive to the comments of other children, they worry about their looks and fear being rejected by their peers. This is normal and should not be criticized. Encourage them to talk about their feelings. Listen to their laments and fears and tell them that you understand how they feel. This helps them increase their self worth. Then make suggestions, sharing your wisdom and life experience. You might say, "Another way of looking at this situation is . . ." or "maybe you want to try . . ." Refrain from being judgmental, from laying down the law, and from uttering "you should". Above all, avoid ridicule, which attacks self esteem and reinforces fears.

SCHOOL AND HOMEWORK

These can become a touchy issue now, especially when the first enthusiasm about them has evaporated. Try to keep your expectations reasonable. You may have missed opportunities in your education but your children cannot make up for that. Instead, be sensitive to the youngsters' needs. After sitting in school all day, they require play and exercise for balance, when possible outdoors. Homework can be addressed later, perhaps after dinner.

Assist with assignments, but be a guide rather than a rescuer. In other words, show how to do the work. Avoid doing it for the child. The latter might get them a good grade for the moment. In the long run, however, it will stunt their independence and hamper their ability to think things through and solve their own problems. Yes, check their homework, but guide them to locate their mistakes by themselves. Then let them find their own solutions.

Do I hear you say "but my kid is too young for this!"? The fact is that humans do their best learning during childhood. Children pick up and retain information more easily than adults. You see, they have not yet split their mind in two. In other words, they are still able to use both their conscious and their subconscious minds, drawing on their intuition as well as their intellect. Being curious and enthusiastic, they have not yet developed resistance to learning. The only thing lacking is judgment based upon life experience. And that is where you can help.

Encourage boys and girls to ask questions, both at home and in school. Keep in touch with teachers, communicating with them directly, rather than through the child. Notices from home to school and vice versa are easily lost or forgotten.

When youngsters bring home reports that they got in trouble at school, refrain from further punishment. Most likely they have already suffered consequences in school. If in doubt, call the school and find out. Double punishment is *not* twice as effective. It will cause the child to become twice as rebellious, however.

During the middle years, children are very conscious of fairness and honesty. When you practice both, they will reward you with their trust. When you don't, they may never trust you again. What a price to pay for being overly zealous!

TAKE AN INTEREST IN SCHOOL

Boys and girls experience school visits by parents and anyone who cares for them as most nurturing. As a family therapist, I made it a practice to visit with my young clients' teachers, principals, school nurses, counselors, etc., at their school. When I made the appointment, I would request that the child, as well as mom or dad, or both, be present during the meeting. If youngsters are to accept ownership of their problems, *they need to be part of the discussion and the resolution.* In my experience, most principals and teachers are quite open to that idea.

Be sure to tell the child in advance what the gathering is about. Go over the agenda again at the start of the meeting, to be sure that it is fresh in everyone's mind. Keep things positive. Describe *in detail,* and with *I statements,* as illustrated in the *feeling talk* earlier in this chapter, the behavior changes you are seeking. Listen to the perceptions and suggestions of the school staff. Be aware of the impact that your appropriate behavior has on your child.

You are demonstrating negotiation skills and how to carry them out. Equally important, you are showing that you are his/her ally. This kind of support will grab the attention of your offspring. Youngsters thrive on loving cooperation among the adults who work with them. If you model blaming and yelling, they are likely to imitate that. When you are respectful and caring, when you explain and negotiate, they will copy those actions instead. Isn't that how you want them to behave?

PRE-PUBERTY

Puberty has been arriving at an ever earlier age in the Western World. It is not unusual for girls to start menstruating at age nine or ten. Pre-puberty, therefore, may start by eight or nine years of age in girls, and only a little later in boys. Since this is the time that hormonal levels start fluctuating, you will notice mood swings in both boys and girls. Normal for this age group, they may continue for several years, through puberty.

MOOD SWINGS

Mood swings are as tough on the youngsters who feel them as they are on their elders. They express themselves as fluctuations between emotional highs and lows. Those who experience them may be exuberant and full of energy one moment, while feeling as though they are dragging themselves through a swamp the next. They appear demanding, irritable, and even angry. Your support and understanding are crucial at this time. You may be tempted to get grouchy, but don't. Use the *feeling talk* instead. Let's try it.

Getting Through Mood Swings with Love

1. Ask the youngster to have a chat with you.
2. Start the conversation with, "I guess you are upset. I can understand how you feel. Why don't we sit down and talk about it?"
3. Express your feelings by means of *the feeling talk,* ending with "I wish you would tell me what this is like for you."
4. Listen; refrain from giving advice at this point.
5. Ask how you can be of help. Perhaps you want to share that you have gone through it too, and have lived through it. Give the child a hug, and say *I love you.*
6. Make yourself available to talk again.
7. Write down your feelings.

Refrain from asking questions that start with why or what. Use statement questions, like "I wonder . . ." instead. If youngsters cannot express feelings verbally, suggest that they draw three pictures, as explained below.

Explain to the child that the first drawing needs to show what the situation feels like now. The second illustrates how it will feel when the problem is resolved. And the third indicates what needs to be done to get from the first to the second. This technique helps those who use it to get their feelings out by putting them on paper, without having to resort to many words. It also guides them to think in terms of a resolution of the problem. Finally, it encourages them to utilize both their intuition and their intellect in getting to a positive outcome. Be sure to discuss the pictures and the feelings that they are portraying with the youngster.

Boys and girls often reject hugs at this time. Some don't like being touched, others want more closeness. Don't take it personally. It's all part of growing up. Safe touching is still important, however, such as patting the child's hand, or putting an arm around his or her shoulders. You might want to offer a hug with "maybe you need a hug right now", or something similar. Avoid pushing that on the youngster, however.

WHAT ABOUT SEX EDUCATION?

Answer questions about sexuality at any time that youngsters pose them. Do so in simple terms at their level of maturity. By age eight, you might start talking about sex more explicitly, since pre-puberty is just around the corner. The next chapter shows, in detail, how to do this.

HAVING FUN

As I said before, children come to playing naturally. They do not have to learn how to do it, if they are emotionally healthy. They even work playfully. Adults, on the other hand, often forget to have fun. This activity is, however, important to our emotional health and all-around balance. If you have forgotten how to do it, observe youngsters at play, without making it obvious that you are watching. Notice that they can be quite serious about what they are doing, even while they are having fun. It is worthwhile for grownups to relearn that skill. Let's see how it's done.

Do It Playfully

1. If you have not yet done so, observe a child at play.
2. Join in the activity, being careful to let the youngster be in charge.
3. Write down your feelings and reactions.
4. Allow yourself play/recreation time before you do your next task.
5. Turn on energetic music that puts you in a playful mood.
6. Give yourself plenty of time, at least an hour.
7. Now go to your task. Notice how you feel and how creative you are.
8. Write down your feelings about that.

Now start another task, but at this time, *do it playfully*. When it is done, write down your insights and feelings.

Would you run your car on a discharged battery? It would not go very far, would it? So, recharge yourself with play between tasks and do your work in a playful rather than a driven fashion. You will have more energy and creativity. Employers are beginning to realize the importance of this principle. More and more provide the opportunity to employees to *recreate* themselves during breaks from the job. They have discovered that it makes good business sense.

FUN TIMES TOGETHER

Make use of every opportunity to engage in family fun together, *now*. Children grow up fast. Once they become teenagers, they lose interest in family activities. Make it a priority to set aside time to play together. Avoid using work as an excuse. You will always be able to do more work, but you can't bring back your offspring's childhood once it is gone. The latest models of toys and computers come and go. What grown-up children remember is the fun times they had with their family during childhood. What memories do you want your youngsters to have?

NINE

Pre-puberty and Puberty: Experimentation and Turbulence

Hey, doesn't anyone like me?
All I ever hear is
"You don't do anything right!"
"Oh, you're so stupid!"
"You're weird!"
Hey, doesn't anyone want me?
If only I'd like myself!
I wish I knew who
I am and where I do belong.
I wish you would just accept me
And love me as I am!
I want to be free,
Be ME!
And love you in my own way!

LATE CHILDHOOD INTO EARLY TEENS

Marked by emotional upheavals, ages ten through fourteen are probably the most challenging years of childhood. As pre-puberty swings into puberty, the war of the hormones causes youngsters to fly high one moment, only to crash the next. Mood swings are the order of the day. Boys and girls may dissolve in tears, burst into angry shouting matches, and break out into sunny smiles, in the space of an hour or less. All of this is as puzzling and disturbing to those experiencing it first hand as it is to the adults who are affected by it.

Peer pressure, fierce by now, can turn cruel. And both boys and girls are highly susceptible to it. To parents, it seems as though every value that they have ever taught their children has been flung into the winds. "My kid, who used to be so bright, doesn't even have a mind of his own any more," they lament, "and the language, I didn't even know these words existed!"

To youngsters, it appears that, no matter what they do, they can't please anyone. If they go along with their peers, their elders get angry and punish them. If they try to live up to their parents' expectations, their peer group gives them a hard time. It is confusing. Most, especially those with the loving support of their families make it through and grow from their experiences. Others capitulate to the greatest pressure, that from their friends. They may turn to nicotine, alcohol, or other drugs to still their pain, or to feel grown up. If this path takes them into crime, it is usually to finance the drug habit. Some children react by withdrawing and becoming depressed, even suicidal. And then there are those who blame their problems on everyone else. Acting alone or joining with like-minded others, they turn to rape and bullets to express their anger and pain.

By the age of ten or eleven years, the differences between boys and girls become quite apparent ~ and not only in physical ways. Girls may become shy and ultra-sensitive to the opinion of others; boys may turn into boisterous showoffs. Self-esteem is now a major issue for both genders. This is hardly surprising, considering all the changes that go on within and outside the youngster.

Many boys and girls become sexually active at this time. "Not my kid!", I can almost hear you exclaim. Perhaps not, but my experience indicates that many engage in sexual activity regularly. Consider the number of teen pregnancies. How do you think those happen?

EMOTIONAL SUPPORT IS CRUCIAL AT THIS TIME

Most experts agree that our value system is formed by age twelve. From then on, youngsters tend to reject parental beliefs and preferences. This can be quite scary to grown-ups. But perhaps, with some effort, you can recall when you did the same thing! This is no time to panic and start throwing your values at your children. Most likely they will not be accepted any way, at this late date, if they have not yet been internalized. If, on the other hand, you have guided them by your example with love and respect all along, young people should have the inner resources to stand up to the pressure from peers ~ when they are ready to do so. You can help by being supportive, lending an *empathetic ear,* and keeping the channels of communication between you and the youngsters *open.* Use the skills you have learned in the earlier sections of this book. Reread those chapters, if necessary.

Give hugs, nurture self esteem, and keep *I love you* statements coming. Refrain from being judgmental. Instead, use the *feeling talk* to express your concern and support. Above all be patient. Be prepared for mistakes to happen and let the youngsters learn from them. Resist the temptation to overreact and over punish, lest you push those leaning toward rebellion into even greater defiance (see the *Stress-Abuse Cycle* in Chapter 1). Be sensitive to the needs of the quiet ones, those who withdraw and hold their feelings in. Youngsters in this volatile age group are prone to moving from depression into despair and hopelessness without warning. If pressured with lengthy grounding, embarrassment in front of peers, or physical/emotional/sexual abuse, they may slip over the brink into suicide attempts. Do you want to be responsible for that?

This is a good time to keep up your interest in school. Continue to consult with teachers regularly. Keep an eye on homework without taking over. As I mentioned before, the key is to guide rather than rescue, encourage rather than control. Being highly sensitive, youngsters in this age group need to be applauded for their successes, no matter how minor. They benefit most from adults who can coach and cheer them on, without cutting them down.

Answer questions honestly. If you don't know the answers, say so, adding that you will try to find them. Or, when appropriate, ask your offspring to look for them. Refer them to places where they can find information, to make it a little easier. By the time I was fourteen years old, I had learned how to think and how to use a library, because there was no one to spoon feed information to me.

Continue to interact with these young people in a loving, understanding, and respectful manner, even while you are setting limits. Let them know by word and deed that you love them. Be available when they come to you with problems. Take the time to sit down with them, to listen, and assist them in working through their problems to resolution. Refrain from trying to fix things for them.

A sound platform for this kind of discussion is the *family council*. This is a family meeting with the specific purpose of keeping communication channels open. It is a good idea to hold it once a week. An opportunity for everyone to voice feelings and receive feedback, the family council is conducted in a democratic manner. All family members, even the little ones, are heard and have equal input. Let's see how that is done.

The Family Council

If you live with a spouse or significant other, discuss with that person your desire to have a family meeting, before speaking to the children. Then figure out, together, how to set it up. Once you are in agreement, invite your children to the meeting. Explain the purpose of the council to them, and set up a time and place that suit *everyone*.

Family Council Meeting

1. Discuss how the meeting will be conducted, state how long it will last, and how problems are to be brought up and resolved.
2. Stay within the time limits and the rules agreed upon.
3. Request that all participants *listen* to each other. Encourage them to use the *feeling talk to state their feelings*. Make sure that everyone has input.
4. Encourage positive feedback to promote understanding and help keep up interest.
5. Show, by your behavior, how to be respectful toward one another.
6. Guide the meeting with love.
7. If a problem cannot be resolved during the allotted time, put it on the agenda for the next meeting.
8. Use your sense of humor, lest things get too heavy.
9. If the Council is a joyous occasion, your children will be motivated to be there for every session. Well, *almost* every time.
10. Ask the participants how they feel about resolving issues in this manner.
11. Schedule the next meeting.
12. Write down your reactions and insights.

During ensuing sessions, experiment with giving each of the youngsters the opportunity to try a rotation as the Chair Person. This is good leadership training. The Chair keeps order, invites participants to state their idea or problem, keeps the discussion flowing, and proposes the date and time for the next meeting.

FUN TIMES TOGETHER

Most preteens and young teens still enjoy family fun as long as it does not interfere with their social life. Don't take this personally. It's not that they don't want to spend time with you. It's just the peer thing. If you crimp their style and keep them away from friends, you will see them wilt. So would you rather have a miserable youngster in your midst, who is there in body only, or a happy kid who really treasures the few hours spent with you because it is well balanced with peer times? Be a good role model by showing that family closeness is a priority for you. Make it fun, and not work, without pressure to attend, and you'll see your child come out of the woodwork to partake, at least part of the time.

ACTIVITIES THAT YOUNG PEOPLE ENJOY

For starters, ask the youngsters what they like to do. Let them have input in the planning of the pastime; that way they will enjoy it more ~ and so will you! Healthy preteens and teenagers usually relish something active, interesting, and a bit out of the ordinary. They get bored easily, you see!

What is a good family activity? Hiking is a delightful sport in which the entire family can participate. I meet hikers on the trail who carry babies in their backpack. And age is no excuse! Trails, ranging from easy through moderate to strenuous, are found almost everywhere. Information and maps are available through the National Park Service and State and County Recreation and Parks Departments. The advantage that hiking has over many other activities is that it is affordable, requiring a minimum of equipment.

If you choose to hike, make sure that you go prepared. Hiking shoes or boots and drinking water are a must. If you don't know the area, get information about it, how strenuous the trails are, how long it takes to walk in and out, what you need to bring, etc. Joining a hiking club would give you the opportunity to walk in a group with experienced hikers who know the trails. Take sunscreen and mosquito repellent, if necessary. And start with *short, easy* hikes in *good* weather until everyone in the family gets into condition. Enjoy!

DISCIPLINE

Children in this age group rarely think of consequences. They need to be reminded that there is such a thing. First, however, face your fears. Notice that I said fears, not anger. You may think that what you are feeling is wrath, but scratch the surface and you will find fear. Who wouldn't be scared when they see their offspring head straight into disaster?

When you are ready to talk, be honest, and state how you feel, using the *feeling talk*. Even teens, who are masters at tuning us out, are shocked into listening when mom or dad talks about their fears with them. "I'm so scared that you will get hurt if you follow this course of action," will more likely grab their attention than, "You idiot, how can you be so stupid!" Go on to discuss the situation and its potential impact, explaining in specific terms the changes that you are looking for.

When a mistake has already been made, consider letting youngsters suffer the consequences of their actions. Think about it! In our society, we are just now learning the repercussions of *not* letting our children experience the results of their misguided actions. Many of those who keep getting into trouble have learned early that they can get away with their behaviors, or that someone will rescue them. Yes, consequences can be painful, but that is also why they are such potent learning experiences. *Make sure,* however, that the situation *is not life threatening and that no one will get injured* as a result. *Only you* can make that decision. When in doubt, discuss it with someone whom you trust.

How do you discipline at this age? One of the most effective ways is still the *brief* total grounding, involving total loss of privileges, as described in Chapter 8. At this age, you can ground one day for normal transgressions, and two days for more serious ones. If you have not used this method before, be sure to explain it with love before the need for it arises. Avoid longer grounding, yelling, taking toys and things away, and physical punishment. All these accomplish is to make young people more rebellious.

TO BE OR NOT TO BE: THE URGE TO END IT ALL

The risk of suicide attempts is great during this volatile period. Given the stress inherent to this cycle, that should not come as a surprise. Both boys and girls are highly sensitive at this time. Any issue, such as being unpopular with peers, feeling unattractive, or not living up to someone's expectations, can place them in peril. Add other stressors to this potent mix, like major losses, perceived failures, unfair punishment, alcohol or drug use, or emotional, physical, or sexual abuse, and you may see youngsters slide over the brink into despair and thoughts of suicide. The risk is especially high when one of their peers commits suicide.

Take all suicidal talk seriously. It may be cryptic, like "life isn't worth living," or, "I can't go on anymore." When you are not sure, *listen* closely. Avoid direct questions. Instead, formulate statement questions, e. g., "I wish you would explain," or, "I wonder how I can be of help." If the youngster seems to have suicidal thoughts, *be supportive* by listening and suggest that it is time to get help. *Do not leave him or her unattended,* while you telephone for assistance. Get in touch with your counselor if you are already working with one, with a psychiatrist, or with a psychiatric hospital. If, however, the child is already attempting suicide, call 911 or other emergency numbers *immediately.* An ambulance can get to you in less time than it would take you to drive to a hospital. Be sure to tell them what is happening, and where you are.

Suicide attempts are frightening. Most youngsters, their family, and their friends experience intense feelings of anger, guilt, and fear after the event. These emotions need to be addressed and worked through immediately with a counseling professional who can work with the whole family. If they are ignored, they may cause long term depression, and potentially, additional suicide attempts.

BODILY CHANGES AND FLUCTUATING MOODS

As you watch with fascination, that little girl who couldn't care less about her appearance turns into a young woman who spends hours in front of the mirror, plastering on makeup until you barely recognize her. She agonizes that her breasts are growing too much or not fast enough, and swoons when some boy, a total stranger to you, calls. What's more, she claims squatting rights to your telephone. Of course you still get to pay the bill!

That cute little guy, who couldn't do enough for you, hardly knows that you exist any more. With eyes and ears only for girls whom you don't even know, he is on the phone with them for hours. You can't get into the bath room, where he is camped in front of the mirror watching his facial hair grow. And he proclaims that he wants to die because his body doesn't grow fast enough ~ or because he is taller than all the other boys.

Looking like their peers and being popular with them are life or death issues to most girls and boys at this time. Being ahead of the crowd is as devastating as lagging behind. As if that is not enough to deal with, their mood fluctuations create monumental frustration both for the young people and their elders.

For your own mental health, remember that these events too shall pass. What you are witnessing is normal behavior during this phase of development. It makes your youngster's passage into adulthood something to look forward to, doesn't it?

More than ever, it is crucial that you take care of yourself, gentle reader. A warm tub bath, followed by meditation will help you to center and calm yourself. Keep your sense of humor about you. Most things are not as terrible as we perceive them to be. When you feel overwhelmed by what you think you see, blink your eyes three or four times, then look again. In many cases, the mountain that you thought you saw shrinks back into the mole hill that it really is.

Another thing that you can do for yourself is to be in touch with Grandmother Earth, so that you can keep yourself firmly grounded in her. Walk among her trees, plants, and rocks, and let them soothe you. Soon you will look at the situation in a more relaxed way.

As for the youngsters, well, more shock waves are awaiting you, so read on.

BUDDING SEXUALITY AND EMOTIONAL NEEDS

As boys and girls develop sexually, their needs diverge in some important ways. Girls tend to become self conscious, boys boisterous. Both reactions have to do with hormones and with feelings of insecurity that develop during this stage. Is that surprising? The territory that these youngsters are entering is totally unfamiliar to them. As their bodies change, so do their perceptions and emotions, all at the same time. If this happened to us grownups, we'd be admitting ourselves to the closest psychiatric unit. Most youngsters and their elders don't know that this is an option. So, everyone just goes on having expectations for the young people to behave appropriately, act with responsibility, excel in school, and somehow inhale all the sexual norms that no one wants to explain to them. Whew, it makes me dizzy just to write about it!

Do you remember what this period was like when you went through it? We might try another exercise here, but let's not. You know what to do. So make yourself as comfortable as possible and take some time to let yourself recall your *own* pre-puberty, and puberty. Meditate on how you can best assist youngsters who go through this experience. Write down your insights, feelings, and plan in your journal.

The stress of this stage makes it difficult for boys and girls to concentrate on tasks. They may become absent-minded and forgetful. School work may suffer, chores may not get done. Self confidence may plummet when youngsters continually compare their bodies to those of others. Take care, however, lest you blame this emphasis on body image on your offspring. Our societal norms have everything to do with it.

This growth phase calls for much patience on the part of grownups. It helps to keep in mind how you react to major stress. Avoid nagging, which is easily tuned out. Instead, use the *feeling talk* to express your feelings and encourage your offspring to do the same. Keep your sense of humor. Some things are best handled in a light vein with a chuckle or two. But *never* laugh at the youngsters. Remember, they are already feeling most vulnerable.

Set priorities. What is more important, getting that chore done, or giving your love and understanding to someone still dependent on you, who is going through a difficult time? Children grow up fast. Before you realize it, they'll be on their own. How do you want them to remember you; as the great yeller? Or maybe as that loving Mom or Dad, or other caring adult, who "was always there for me"?

Sexual development brings with it the pressure to become sexually active. All this can be quite overwhelming to parents. Should you let your children date? What is the right age for them to start dating? How do you handle it when you find out that your child is sexually active at the tender age of eleven or twelve?

TALKING ABOUT SEX

The fact is that many boys and girls do become sexually active at this time. You will not find that they volunteer this information to their elders, however. Questioning them just causes them to clam up. A better way is to sit down with them and discuss openly your values regarding love and sex. Explain things at their level of understanding. Do it lovingly and honestly. This is your opportunity to give your child an introduction to *the emotional and spiritual aspects* of love and sex. Make it as comfortable and laid-back a conversation as you can.

If you are uncomfortable talking about sex, deal with your feelings before the discussion. Become more informed about the subject, if necessary. Numerous texts are available on the topic.

Sexuality is a beautiful part of life, a gift from the Creator, and we all own it. If you have not yet had that sex talk with your son or daughter, now is the time. Many youngsters are well into pre-puberty by age ten, and in puberty by eleven. I'm sure that you want them to be prepared.

Plan to encourage your listeners to ask questions. Respond honestly, at their level of maturity. Avoid giving more detail than they are ready to handle. If you don't know the answer, tell them that you will find it, and get back to them.

Ideally, both parents are involved in this conversation. It is important that *male and female* views be represented for children of *both genders*. Take your time. You don't need to do it all at once. It may be easier on you and the youngster to have several discussions. It is time to stop denying and delaying the issue, however. If you wait too long, your child may interrupt you with "Aw, I already know all that stuff!" The earlier you start, the simpler it is to teach the values that are important to you, in a gentle piece-by-piece approach.

To plan a discussion about sex, talk with your spouse or partner, if available, *before* you sit down with your daughter or son. Come to an agreement with each other regarding the time and place of the meeting; the content of the discussion; and how it will be conducted. Choose a location that is comfortable for all of you.

Resolve to make this a *positive* occasion. Your child will remember it for many years. When you speak with your offspring, issue an invitation to attend the event, rather than an order. Explain the purpose of the meeting. Be flexible in the scheduling. Pre-teens are super busy people in our time.

Now prepare for your talk by writing down your fears, concerns, and plans.

You will find an outline of a discussion about love and sex below. Taylor it to your own needs and those of your youngster.

Let's Talk About Love and Sex

1. At the beginning of the session, introduce the topic, using *I statements* from the *feeling talk*.
2. Before beginning your presentation, welcome questions about love and sex.
Listen with care.
3. Answer those questions first.
4. Tailor your talk to the maturity level of your youngster. Pause frequently for questions and comments.
5. When done, sum up briefly what was said.
6. Invite your child to come to you with questions. Add that it was good to have this talk, and that you might want to do it again.
7. Write down your feelings and insights.

Should people other than parents teach children about love & sex? Teachers, counselors, and health professionals who are qualified to teach this subject may do so, as may anyone delegated by parents. When parents are willing and available, I ask them to do it themselves, however. To me it is a parent's privilege, part of their participation with the Creator in the act of creation.

PREVENTING EARLY TEEN PREGNANCIES

When you guide children with unconditional love, you remove their reasons for becoming sexually active at too early an age. Premature sexual involvement is more about low self-esteem than about sexual desire. Girls and boys will turn to someone for love, when they feel rejected by someone. The leap into sexual love is easy when you feel unloved, emotionally insecure, and sexually confused.

Educating children about sex, and letting them know that pregnancy is a natural consequence of unprotected sexual activity, is another way to practice prevention. If you believe in abstinence, teach them about it. If you want your youngsters to learn about contraceptives, instruct them in their use. It's up to you. At this point you still have some influence.

If you care about your sons and daughters, teach them how to protect themselves against sexually transmitted diseases. You may save their lives. HIV and Aids are a reality, and are easier to prevent than to treat. Check with your health professional or your local Aids Association how to counsel your teen about this.

DEALING WITH PREGNANCY

Unconditional loving is the best way to be supportive if your child becomes pregnant. The new parents and their child need and deserve all the love and support that you can give them, for all the reasons outlined at the beginning of this book, and more. Pregnancy at this early age is frightening to boys as well as girls. Usually, they know that they are not ready for this, even though they may not admit it. Facing difficult decisions, they need a loving adult who is available to listen, and willing to guide them with love.

This is a good time to turn to the Creator for your own guidance. Turn over any burden that you feel, release your fears and clear yourself, and ask for guidance. Communication with the parent(s) of the other person involved in the pregnancy is important. Suggest a *family council* for all of you, using the basic steps described on page 82. Make sure that the young couple is included, so that they will have input into the decision-making process.

Consult a qualified family therapist early on. This is a time when the families of the young parents-to-be need to get together, to rally round, to be loving and supportive to the couple. Since families in this situation are rarely in the mood for dialog with each other, they may need an outsider who is skilled in family communication to assist them. A family therapist can do that for you. Reread the first few chapters of this book. Put the needs of the infant above your own, to give it a good start in life.

Write down your insights, feelings, and inspirations.

CHALLENGES AND OPPORTUNITIES OF LATE CHILDHOOD

Granted, this is a difficult period for everyone involved. But it is also an opportunity for the family to act as a team. The challenges and temptations which children face are part of life. They are always present. Guide your offspring with unconditional love and respect, and you will create an environment in which they can learn from these experiences. Thus you make it possible for them to stretch toward their potential. And as they grow, so do you. Is there a better way to assist youngsters in making a successful transition into the late teens and from there into adulthood?

TEN

Post-Puberty: The Roller Coaster Years

I am ME!
A child no more!
I'm on my path,
Well, almost there.
Don't hold me back.
Respect me,
And I will honor you!
Oh, yeah,
I need your love.
And though I may not show it,
I really love you too.

ADOLESCENCE: AGE FIFTEEN TO EIGHTEEN

To the adolescent, navigating through the late teens feels like a ride on a roller coaster. Exhilarating highs alternate with sudden lows that are every bit as scary as the spooky elevator drop at the Tower of Terror in Orlando, Florida. Hormones, peer pressure, the need to rebel, and fluctuating self-esteem still exert much pressure on the individual.

CHANGE IS THE ORDER OF THE DAY.

Fighting change only leads to ulcers or worse, so you may as well accept it with as much grace as you can muster. Expect your teenager to appear totally rational and reasonable one day, and like a visitor from another planet the next. True, adolescents do have concern for their poor aging elders who aren't quite with it. Sometimes they will even show it. Mostly, they just turn up their noses in disgust. Or they make us aware of their opinion in the highest decibels to ensure that the entire neighborhood hears how hopelessly unfit we are as parents.

RIGHT NOW, RUNNING AWAY TO A MONASTERY SEEMS LIKE A GOOD IDEA

The situation seems hopeless. At any rate, we're too exhausted to even try to get through this. To make matters worse, youngsters skillfully play one parent against the other, especially if they don't live under the same roof, or if one of them is a step parent. But relax, all is not lost. Rather, for this age group this state of affairs is status: normal.

As a therapist, I am concerned when teenagers do not rebel at least to some extent. Adolescence is the age of defiance. If rebellion is not expressed openly, it is internalized. The unexpressed anger and frustration then build into rage. Some adolescents blame themselves, becoming depressed, even suicidal. Others run away from home. And some, as we have witnessed, burst like volcanoes and express their rage with bullets. Those reactions would impact on the youngsters and you for years to come! Is that worth it?

SURVIVING AND THRIVING

Fortunately there is something that you can do to prevent the dire consequences that I described above. In the morning when you get up, take a large glass, fill it with unconditional love, sprinkle a handful of patience and a good pinch of empathy on top, and stir well. Drink the contents slowly and with appreciation. Make sure that you enjoy the glow when it reaches your heart. Say to yourself *I love you!* Then move into your day.

You can live through the adolescence of your offspring with *patience, understanding, humor,* and *unconditional love.* Try to recall your own teen years. *Did you not rebel?* It is so tempting to handcuff the youngsters, but definitely not a good idea. Instead, sit down together. Find out what is going on by *listening.* Express your love in words. Use your wisdom to guide your teen, without taking over. Use the *feeling talk.* Keep all channels of communication open. And take care of yourself with meditation, prayer, exercise, grounding yourself in nature, etc., as described in previous chapters.

Do you recall how you can stop yourself from overreacting? Let's try that as an exercise.

Calming Yourself and Fine Tuning Your Attitude

1. Emotionally step back from your situation and take a look at it.
2. Draw in an easy breath through your nose, and then exhale slowly.
3. From now on, focus on exhaling ever more slowly.
4. Letting the inhaling take place automatically, exhale slowly, *very* slowly, through your open mouth.
5. Inhaling again, exhale even more slowly.
6. Repeat this step three more times; slowing each exhaled breath even more.
7. Blink your eyes *three* times.
8. Now look at the situation again. How does it seem to you now?
9. Enter your feelings in your journal.

The breathing exercise above is based on an exercise in *HEALING INTO IMMORTALITY* by Gerald Epstein, MD. Coupled with the eye-blinking that I have added, it can empower you to change your perception. Now you can once again utilize your coping skills and function as a rational adult.

EMOTIONAL NEEDS OF MATURING TEENAGERS

Adolescents need more space and privacy than their juniors. If at all possible, they should have their own room. They need time alone, so don't be surprised if they keep to themselves quite a bit. Expect them to want to spend less time with family, more with friends. Their choices of clothing, hair style and music are most likely quite different from yours. Weren't you in that space not too long ago???

Give these young people your respect. It is quite simple, at least to them: *respect me and I'll respect you*. Refrain from treating them like children. They really are young men and women. Request their input into decisions that affect them and others in the family. You will all benefit. Teens often see things as they are. They have creative ideas. Avoid being judgmental, or authoritarian, unless you wish to lose their trust. The rule of thumb is always to *listen, listen, listen* and telling them that you love them.

How do you listen to and talk with teenagers? Let's find out.

Communicating With Adolescents

1. Discuss the situation with your spouse or partner.
2. Develop a strategy. It is very important that both of you be on the same wave length.
3. Invite your teen to meet with both of you at a mutually agreeable time and explain the purpose of the get-together.
4. At the beginning of the session, reiterate the purpose.
5. Employing the *feeling talk*, state your case. Avoid blaming.
6. Invite the young person to speak, also using the feeling talk.
7. Listen! Resist the temptation to give advice.
8. Ask the adolescent how he or she would resolve this situation. Listen.
9. Give your feedback, staying with suggestions and filling in of gaps, rather than telling what to do.
10. Together, discuss how to implement any changes to be made.
11. Suggest a target date by which the situation is *expected* to be resolved.
12. Schedule a meeting shortly after the target date to review progress.
13. Be sure to say *I love you*. Offer a hug, but let it go if it is refused.
14. Write down your feelings and insights.

Family councils, including the entire family, are still appropriate. From time to time, especially when there is need for privacy for the adolescent, it may be necessary to meet with him or her without family members other than those in a parenting position.

THE DRIVE TO REBEL

It appears to be a natural law that the icons of the generation in power be called into question by every new generation coming along. And adolescence seems to be the appointed time frame. Defiance is the norm for this age group, so much so, that the lack of it can slow a youngster's emotional development. Questioning authority is part of the individuation process. In other words, in order to become emotionally mature individuals who can stand on our own two feet, we need to rebel at some time in our lives. This is a good age for that to happen. You disagree? Consider the alternative: If not in adolescence, then when?

Those who were kept from talking back and resisting their elders as teenagers, tend to start rebelling in their middle years, when they finally feel strong enough to do so. It is then called *mid-life crisis*. And a *crisis* it is, one of major proportions. By then, people are well into their careers, usually in responsible positions, and have dependents and mortgages. In other words, they have much to lose. The impact on the individual, and on those who depend on him or her, can be disastrous and may last many years. Everything that acts upon one person in the family affects everyone else as well. Therefore this delayed rebellion influences the next generation too. Is that better?

Let teenagers get the defiance out of their system now. Encourage them to talk it out. It will be over before you know it. And, when you raise youngsters with unconditional love, their rebelliousness will be relatively brief and mild.

GENDER ISSUES

While many of the pressures on adolescents are similar for boys and girls, others vary according to gender. For hundreds of generations we have looked to our males to be tough and macho. Now we expect them to be sensitive and gentle. Yet they had better be tough as well, lest they get teased, even beaten mercilessly by their peers.

We have long expected females to be strong, and to run business and country while wars were being waged. When the men got back, the women were forced to vacate the jobs which they had filled so well. Though things have improved, some girls and boys are still discouraged from entering careers that are deemed inappropriate for their gender.

Double messages about gender roles are absorbed by our children from infancy on. Those youngsters who dare to be different get ostracized or punished for stepping out of line. Others develop the need to conform and become driven to do everything that is expected of them, perfectly. They become the top students and the hardest workers, and yet it never seems to be good enough. They literally wear themselves out trying even harder. Some go on to become depressed, others develop asthma, allergies, headaches, or other chronic conditions that reflect pain, anger, and fears held inside. Many lose themselves in alcohol and other drugs.

The pressure to succeed reaches a crescendo in late adolescence. It is as if the world of grownups wants to make sure that teenagers learn all their lessons and be more successful than their elders, all at the same time; even if it kills them. Sadly, these demands, impossible to live up to, do kill youngsters. Some die slowly. The constant stress of trying to live up to unrealistic expectations fosters nicotine, alcohol and drug abuse. When that abuse becomes dependence and is sustained long enough, it can lead to severe illness and premature death. Strain on the circulatory system, overdoses, drug interactions, accidents, suicide, and murder, all may cut an individual down instantly. *What are we doing to our offspring?*

HOW YOU CAN HELP

You have the power to put a stop to overtaxing your precious children. First of all, sort out your own gender role expectations. Have you been giving children double messages? Put clear communication in its place. Invite your teen to a dialog of the issue. Be forthright. State where you have been coming from and what you intend to do about it. Listen to the youngster's input. Perhaps you can put your heads and hearts together and come up with a resolution.

Next, take an honest look at *your* life. Do you have expectations for perfection from yourself, your children, others? Do you feel unfulfilled, dissatisfied? If you do, work with yourself to change that. Avoid taking it out on others. If you have lost a part of yourself in the shuffle of life and making a living, *find your true self*. It's there, somewhere underneath all that need to please others, deep under those layers of anger, guilt, shame, and fear that have accumulated over the years. Once you release and let go of all those negative feelings, you will find a beautiful person, *your self*. Yes, it is important that you do that. How can you hope to help youngsters find their way, if you are still lost?

Use the releasing/letting go exercises that I have taught you earlier in this volume. Be sure to release and let go of unreasonable expectations for yourself, your offspring, and your spouse, as well.

Children of all ages copy adult behaviors. Your example is a powerful teaching tool. When you act with responsibility and treat youngsters with love and respect, they learn to be respectful, loving, and responsible, in turn. When you take care of yourself by releasing and letting go of negative habits and feelings, you are giving yourself the gift of balance and harmony. Adolescents will notice not only your action, but also what it does for you. And, with time, they may even do the same for themselves.

Refrain from nagging and bickering when you want your teen to do chores. The *feeling talk* works so much better! State your need clearly ~ and do not expect an immediate response. Power struggles, the need to be controlling and pushy, only escalate into worse behaviors. Ultimately you will end up pushing your child away! Is that what you want?

Instead, say that you need it done some time today, but leave the exact time open. Most tasks are not that urgent, are they? What is more important to you, getting *things* done immediately, or having a close *relationship* with your child? Go ahead and have a good laugh when things get too serious. Humor and laughing are good medicine! And remember to keep the *I love you's* coming.

The rest will fall into place. You will know what to do, because you have been there yourself. Do it gently, without pushing.

BOUNDARIES AND LIMIT SETTING

Always important, boundaries and limits need to be tailored to the age and maturity of the young person. Adolescents can stay out later at night, but a curfew is still necessary. Rather than fighting peer pressure, a losing battle anyway, use it. Talk to the parents of your children's friends. Negotiate a curfew time that works for all of you. You will eliminate one sure source of friction. Explain the limits that you are setting to the youngsters and adhere to them. Follow through with action immediately.

Too many rules escalate rebelliousness. So stick to several juicy ones that are really important to you. Have and express the firm expectation that they will be followed. Allow questions and discussion, (A.K.A. talking back), but adhere to the boundaries that you have set. *I understand your feelings, but I still expect you to do this*, said firmly, will go a long way. If limits have outlived their usefulness, push the delete button! Before you do that, be sure to notify everyone, including the other parent, *and* the adolescent, to prevent confusion and frustration down the road.

AGE-APPROPRIATE CONSEQUENCES

Obviously time out is out of the question at this age. Long grounding or taking things away, make adolescents more rebellious. Most adults and teens report that total restrictions of short duration work much better. Let's try that.

Total grounding is set up for *one* day. All privileges, including phone calls by or to friends, television, radio, stereo, etc., are removed. There is no going out, other than to school, job, or church, and no visits by friends. Homework and chores are still expected to be done. *Do* continue to communicate in a loving way with the youngster, however. The consequences are for negative *behaviors*. If you attack the *person*, it will affect self esteem and cause more problems. As my grandmother used to say, *what you call out into the forest, is what you get echoed back*. If the transgression warrants it, consider adding an atonement task, such as cleaning the toilet. It will get your teen's attention more surely than would longer grounding. The task is only as long in duration as you have time to supervise. Consider an hour. And don't expect perfection. The chore is over when time is up, even if it is not finished.

To make this method more effective, set it into motion immediately after the misbehavior, or the next day at the latest. Adolescents tend to have short memories. Of course, any change in consequences needs to first be discussed with your spouse or partner, as well as with your offspring.

PARTIES

Adults should be present to supervise parties until adolescents are *eighteen* years old. In this country you are responsible for the actions of your sons and daughters until then. Be aware of what they are doing without being heavy handed about it. Insist that your offspring go only to those parties where a parent or parent surrogate is present. Any hassles you might get in the short term because of this rule are well worth it in terms of long-term peace of mind.

ALCOHOL AND DRUG USE

Teach your children to observe the laws of your state regarding the use of alcohol and other drugs. When you guide and discipline them with unconditional love, have reasonable expectations, set appropriate limits, and teach them about consequences, you are helping to prevent problems.

Some youngsters, however, are influenced by friends to try drugs. Supervise adolescents in the choice of friends. Make it a habit to meet them and their parents. When your teens go out, find out where they will be and when they will return. Get telephone numbers. When *you* go out, let them know the same.

GETTING HELP FOR YOUNGSTERS WITH DRUG PROBLEMS

If you suspect that your adolescent has an alcohol or drug problem, get him or her help, *at once*. The longer you wait, the worse it becomes. *It will not go away by itself.* And remember, *nicotine* is a harmful drug too.

There are numerous good alcohol and drug treatment programs all over the country. They are listed in the Yellow Pages of your telephone book. The Family Services or Social Services Department of your county can give you information about them. Treatment centers, mental health centers and many churches and newspapers publish the meeting places and times of support groups like Alcoholics Anonymous, Al-Anon, Alateen, Nar-Anon, Adult Children of Alcoholics, Cocaine Anonymous, Nicotine Anonymous, Codependents Anonymous, etc. The telephone numbers of these services are usually listed in the white pages of the telephone book as well. These programs will also give you information on how to recognize substance abuse in your loved one.

HOW CAN YOU TELL WHETHER A TEENAGER IS DEPRESSED?

Teens are concerned about their looks, so they may not *seem* depressed in terms of physical appearance. What *may* indicate depression is lack of motivation and energy, fatigue, excessive sleeping, overeating or loss of appetite, lack of cleanliness, or loss of interest in keeping their room neat and clean. The youngster may appear to be lazy. Other red flags are a drop in grades at school and refusing to participate in social activities that the person used to enjoy.

WHAT CAN YOU DO TO HELP?

Start with *I love you* and the offer of a hug. If you suspect depression, don't wait for things to get worse. Take your child to a qualified mental health practitioner, preferably one who works with adolescents, for an evaluation. If you are a care or service provider to the youngster, recommend to the parents that they do so. When teenagers talk about wanting to end it all, *always take it seriously* and *get help at once*.

SUICIDE RISK

What I said in Chapter Nine bears repeating here. Given the high stress, pressure, and need to obsess that is a hallmark of this age group, the risk for suicide is great. When additional factors, like major losses, perceived failures, over-punishment, alcohol or drug use, or emotional, physical, or sexual abuse, come to bear, teens frequently think of suicide as an escape. The risk is especially high when one of their peers commits suicide.

Take all suicidal talk *seriously*, even if you have heard it before and it did not happen. Sometimes it is cryptic, like "life isn't worth living," or "I can't go on anymore." Listen closely. Avoid direct questions and *you should* advice. Make statement questions, e. g., "I wish you would explain" or "I wonder how I can be of help." Then listen again. Avoid ridicule, or pushing.

If the adolescent seems to have suicidal thoughts, *be supportive* by listening and suggest that it is time to get help. *Do not leave him or her unattended*, while you telephone for assistance. Get in touch with your counselor, if you are already working with one, with a psychiatrist, or with a psychiatric hospital. If, however, the individual is already attempting suicide, *call emergency services*, such as *911, immediately*. If available, it is better to go that route, because an emergency service can start working on the individual as soon as they arrive, and can get to to a hospital faster than you could. Be sure to tell them what is going on, and where you are located.

Suicide attempts are frightening for everyone. Most young people, their family, and their friends have intense feelings of anger and guilt after the event. These *emotions need to be addressed* and worked through immediately with a counseling professional who can work with the whole family. If they are ignored, they may cause long term depression, and, potentially, additional suicide attempts.

TEEN SEX AND PREGNANCY

Please review the sections on sex and pregnancy in Chapter 9. Though some may abstain on moral principles, many adolescents in this age group are sexually active. If you have raised your teen with love, you will probably be aware of it, if he or she becomes sexually involved with someone. The closer your relationship is with your children the more likely they will trust you with such information.

What can you do about it? Not much. You are dealing with an individual who is nearly an adult with his or her own ideas about this most private of areas. If you think you can police teenagers, good luck! It's a 24-hour per day job! The Creator has endowed adolescent males with an explosive sex drive at this prime time of their lives. Many young females, though not yet at their own sexual prime, are quite happy to join them in sexual exploration.

You can, however, continue the sex talks that you have started years ago. If you care about your sons and daughters, teach them how to prevent pregnancy, and how to protect themselves against sexually transmitted diseases. You may save their lives. HIV and Aids are a reality, and they are easier to prevent than to treat. Check with your health professional or with your local aids association on how to counsel your teen about this.

If you have religious concerns about the prevention of pregnancy, discuss them with your minister, priest, pastoral counselor, or spiritual advisor. Be aware that prevention is easier and far less invasive than abortion. And while you may be against abortion, your youngster may not share your concern, especially while engaged in sexual passion. All too frequently, young people come to see counselors and family therapists, with or without parents, *after* abortion, if they come at all. Typically, they have rushed into a decision that will have major impact on their lives, without much forethought. The aftermath was not considered, consequences were not discussed. Whether or not to remain pregnant *is a choice that a person of this age and level of maturity should not have to make.*

If an abortion has already taken place, refrain from blaming and being judgmental. Contact your daughter's physician for a physical examination to make sure that no harm was done, as well as a counselor, family therapist, or pastoral counselor, at *once*. The risk of depression and suicide attempts is very high at this time. *Get help now.*

ADOLESCENCE IS A TIME OF GROWTH

Most adolescents are good people. Once you listen to them, you will find that they really care. There are many wondrous things happening during this stage of development. If you can accept the inherent changes, and remind yourself to act with unconditional love, a whole new relationship can open up between you and your teenager. When you open your heart, as well as your eyes, you will see the personality of your beloved young person unfold and mature. Do you recall your excitement when you watched the same child move forward self propelled, in infancy? Recapture that sense of rapture and awe, and rejoice with the young people as they move forward into adulthood.

In many tribal cultures on Grandmother Earth this time is welcomed and celebrated by the entire tribe. Prepared by the adults, the young people go off alone, on vision quests, to learn their purpose in this life. Upon their return, they are honored in ancient rites, and welcomed into the circle of grownups. In Western traditions, we have graduations and confirmations, but somehow they seem to have lost their deeper meanings. How do we encourage our young to find their purpose in life? Too many of us are still trying to locate our own path in our middle years and beyond! Can we afford that waste of talent?

This is a time to celebrate, to focus on the wonder of it all. It is time to accept teenagers as whole persons, without worrying about age and generational differences. How about *a feast to mark their entry into adulthood* with all its privileges and responsibilities? Congratulate them ~ and yourself, for having made it this far. Sing with them, dance with them, laugh with them, tell them that you love them, and hug them ~ if they'll let you!

ELEVEN

Dealing With Life's Curve Balls

Life is not always
As we would like it to be.

We have focused on the needs of parents and children under fairly routine circumstances, so far. As we walk through life, however, we may be tossed out of our comfortable groove. Like it or not, change lurks just around the corner. Loved ones move on and pass on. Major illness, divorce, financial problems, addictions, abuse, can happen to anyone. Natural disasters may touch our lives. Wars decimate and tear families apart all over the world.

Though they cause us discomfort, major change and the crisis that it precipitates are opportunities to help us grow. They may force us to face something that we have not been willing to see. Or they present a chance to purge a trait, like too much dependence on someone or something. Crisis provides us with the opportunity to move to a higher spiritual plane. Seizing it is our choice. That is what life is about.

GROWING THROUGH CRISIS

Much as elevators take us from one floor to another, crisis can offer us transition from one level of our spiritual development to the next. Fear this shift, or fight it, and you get more mess, more stress. Expect and accept it, and you will profit from a growth experience that will help you move forward on your path.

Though you may not like periods of transition, though you may go to pieces before you do anything else, *you can survive it all and grow* from it. Let's consider some ways to do that.

CRISIS AS OPPORTUNITY: STRETCHING YOURSELF SPIRITUALLY

Major transitions may produce losses that translate into crises. At any time, we may lose everyone we love, everything we possess. Nevertheless, we hate to let go of anyone, anything. In our possession-oriented culture, we forget that children, people, and belongings are ours on loan, from the Creator. So we walk through life, expecting everything to last, and everyone to stick around. Is that realistic?

Open your eyes! This is a world of temporaries. People leave us, loved ones pass on. We may lose health, wealth, youth, physical beauty, our home, relationships, pets, businesses, careers. It's all part of living in material form, on this planet. These very losses with their attending crises, however, are opportunities to learn to *let go, let God*. It may be difficult to see at first, but you can turn what you think of as deprivation, into *spiritual gain*. It is your choice. When you elect to exercise your freedom to let go, and turn over to the Creator what you cannot change, you actually become more independent. An essential ingredient in the growth process, autonomy helps you expand yourself spiritually.

The first reaction to loss is grief. Though everyone does not show it, and many fight it, all who are capable of feeling, experience this sorrow. If you have pets living with you, you know that they too mourn, as indeed do many animals.

When we sustain several losses at once, we tend to plunge into one grief reaction after another. Take, for example, the impact of divorce on the family. First, there is the loss of the love relationship between the parents. Then family stability is interrupted as one parent moves out and is no longer readily available to the children. Financial losses may be incurred. The family home may have to be sold with an ensuing move, and possibly a drop in living standard. Several major stressors, in one stroke, suddenly descend upon the family! Is it surprising then, that adults have breakdowns and children develop behavior problems as a result of divorce?

Events that cause losses are called *stressors*. Frequently referred to as stress, the response to loss is actually *mourning* over losing someone or something important. Our sense of future can cause us much grief in terms of *anticipated losses*, i.e., losses that have not yet happened. A similar reaction is brought about by *perceived* deprivation, or thinking that something or someone significant is being taken from us.

Whatever the cause, grief needs to be worked through and expressed, lest you sink into it ever more deeply. Usually involving denial, anger, sadness, guilt, shame, and fear, unexpressed mourning causes those blockages to the flow of love that I described earlier.

This wall of negative feelings can become impenetrable to the point of interfering with relationships with all others. Indeed, in my experience, it is a common, albeit unrecognized, cause of the breakdown of relationships, especially marriages.

Yes, you are entitled to your feelings. And no, you do not have to hold on to them. To help you release them, talk to someone who knows how to listen, a friend, minister, or counselor. Or write a letter, *which you are not going to send*, to the person you have lost, or to God, expressing your emotions honestly. It is permissible to address individuals who have passed on, as though they were still with you. This is primarily *for you*, to help you put closure on the situation, so that you can get on with your life. Avoid rereading what you have written, to prevent reabsorbing those feelings. Be sure to destroy the letter. Then perform the exercises that you have learned previously, to release and let go of the grief. Be sure to replace it with love, lest more negative emotions step into the void.

It is possible that these exercises do not give you the relief that you are seeking. They may bring up feelings that you have previously repressed. If this is the case, and especially if you have been piling grief on top of unresolved mourning, seek the assistance of a member of the clergy, a counselor, or a family therapist. Make sure that they have expertise in *bereavement counseling*.

KILLER GRUDGES

Some people become so embroiled in their pain and anger over a loss, that they refuse to let go. They turn their feelings into bitterness, anger that is held onto for a long time. Bearers of grudges often refuse to communicate with those whom they hold responsible for their loss. This may go on for the rest of their lives.

A challenge to all who are affected by them, grudges are most unhealthy for their owners. These individuals are literally bearing a burden, a load that seems to expand and grow over time. Left unresolved, it is capable of causing major emotional problems, chronic physical pain, and sickness. In the long run, it can lead to terminal illness and death.

Some take out their buried anger violently on people who had nothing to do with the event leading up to it. They may not even know these parties. News reports are filled with such incidents. Though apparently random, such acts are usually the legacy of grudges that their owners have allowed to fester until they erupt in unbridled fury.

It is crucial that bitterness and resentment be released and let go of as quickly as possible.

HOW TO RELEASE GRUDGES.

Get in touch with the feeling that underlies your inability to let go. Is it fear? *Admit* to that emotion, let yourself feel it. Next, *detach* from the sensation, take a step back emotionally. If you have difficulty doing that, look up at the starry sky at night. Try to find the patterns that they form. See yourself in relation to the stars, and then consider your fear, anger, etc., again. Look for the pattern in those feelings. What does it tell you about yourself?

Sit down with the partner to your grudge and verbalize your pain and anger, using the *feeling talk*. If much weight has accumulated in your burden, you may want to practice first, and to write your emotions in the form of a letter which you will not send. Forgive, first yourself, then the other person, as described in Chapter 2, by saying to yourself, *I forgive myself and all others for this distraction from the light,*. Then release and let go with *I am releasing and letting go of . . .* , plugging in the negative feeling. Fill yourself with love for yourself and for the ones you have forgiven.

Write down your emotions and insights.

WHEN CHILDREN GRIEVE

Though rarely given credit for it, youngsters are deeply affected by stress and grief. Indeed, children are more vulnerable than adults in crisis situations. Innocent bystanders hurt by the decisions and actions of grownups, they are the last to find out what is happening; and they lack the power to shape events. Many experience guilt when their families split up or when loved ones pass on. Some withdraw and become depressed, others act out their feelings of fear, anger, sadness, and guilt. Memory is impaired, as is the ability to concentrate. When that happens, teachers and parents tend to overreact. Disruptive students are punished, not only in school, but, just for good measure, again by their parents! Or they are diagnosed to be learning-disabled without a thorough evaluation, and placed on medication to control their behavior. Youngsters who are affected by family stress and grief should be referred to child therapists or family counselors. Crises can be most frustrating for children and adults alike. When grownups are caught up in their own loss and grief, they find it difficult to muster empathy for the situation of the youngsters. The latter, on the other hand, are typically still reacting when their parents are already recovering. Moms and dads then want to go on with their lives. Failing to comprehend that their offspring aren't ready to do the same, they advise them to *get over it!* Is it easy to do that? How would you feel if someone said that to you while you are wrestling with emotions that seem to pull you into a dark hole from which you see no escape?

Other dynamics may develop. Youngsters may mourn out of sympathy when a family member, to whom they are close, gets stuck in unresolved grief. Ever sensitive to the feelings of grownups, they may take them on and become depressed as well. Or they may step into the roles vacated by non-functioning grownups, taking over their responsibilities. In both cases, the consequences for the child can be serious. Much time and money is spent on therapy by adult survivors of such childhood events.

Please see below what you can do to assist boys and girls during their time of mourning.

HELPING CHILDREN WITH THEIR SORROW

Your emotional support and understanding are most important. This is a time for unconditional loving and lots of hugging. Refrain from being critical or judgmental. *Lower your expectations* in terms of grades; ability to concentrate; doing chores; and personal appearance. Be sure to tell mourning youngsters often that you love them and that you relate to their feelings. Encourage them to weep. Tears release pent-up emotions and their biochemical byproducts.

Even outgoing boys and girls may become shy when they grieve. They may refuse to socialize. Many have a natural affinity for animals, however. You might want to get a pet for the support it offers. Make sure that it is gentle and that it likes to be held. Discuss this with your child first, however, and involve him or her in the selection of the animal.

Open communication is crucial. Children do best when they are kept informed about stressful events that affect the adults around them. Talk with them when someone is gravely ill or dying, when you are considering separation or divorce, or when you are in a financial crisis. Uncertainty is a major stress event. Being kept in the dark causes youngsters greater stress than learning the bad news. You will find your offspring more understanding of your situation, when you let them know what is going on, in terms that they can comprehend.

Boys and girls are resourceful and, given the opportunity, have something to contribute to the resolution of a problem. Listen to them. Even little ones can see things quite clearly. Who was it anyway that said, "The emperor isn't wearing any clothes"? Youngsters are less likely to go into denial than adults.

A good way to communicate is in regular family meetings, like the *family council* described in Chapter Nine. Make sure that everyone is invited, even the little ones. Children are more cooperative when they are part of this process.

It is crucial that everyone in the family take good care of themselves during periods of crisis. Nurture yourselves physically as well as emotionally, get regular exercise, healthful nutrition, and sufficient sleep. Talk about your grief; let yourself cry when tears come.

This is a good time for the whole family to get out into nature. Take frequent walks among plants, flowers, and trees. The energy and color that these beings share so freely are very healing. Release your sadness, anger, guilt, fears to the Creator.

GET HELP!

One of the most effective steps that you can take is to ask for assistance when you or the youngsters in your charge need it.

There are many helpful organizations that devote their time and effort to assisting youngsters and grownups in working through their losses. Some specialize in guiding those who have become widowed, or are going through separation or divorce; others help with the loss of children.

Rainbows International Grief Support Organization for Children is a support group that assists children who are grieving the loss of a loved one through death, divorce, or other transitions. You may contact Rainbows through churches and schools, by email at *info@rainbows.org*, or call 1-800-266-3206. Their web site is *www.rainbows.org*

Numerous other organizations are standing by to assist you. Since they vary from one community to another, I cannot tell you who they are. You can locate them via your county, churches, mental health centers, health and mental health professionals, your local Public Library, or the Yellow Pages.

If you need more intensive assistance, consider spiritual or family counseling. When your family gets together to consult a professional during tough times, your offspring get the message that you care about them. It removes the burden of feeling helpless from their shoulders. They realize that your family is able to resolve the problem, and that it is all right to ask for help. And while counseling requires an investment of effort, time, and money, it greatly speeds up recovery. *The only thing more costly is doing nothing.*

ASSISTING YOUNGSTERS WITH DISABILITIES

Whether your offspring are challenged physically, mentally, emotionally, or developmentally, *they are always children first*. Everything that I have taught you about meeting the needs of youngsters applies to those who live with special challenges, as well. The key is to focus on the child, not the disability. Give your love with compassion and support. Avoid pity and treating this individual differently from your other children. Have *appropriate* expectations. And give lots of hugs and I love you's to every one of your offspring.

Normally it is not the youngsters who have a problem with their special challenges. They may see them as an opportunity to learn something, or to work something out. A learning disability can enlighten you about the need for patience, for example. A physical restriction can help you learn to ask for and accept assistance from others. Experiencing emotional challenges can teach you more about empathy than can any one who has not been there.

Parents and others who provide care to disabled children may have difficulty accepting the situation. Take a look inside yourself, *with great love and honesty*. How do you feel about the special challenge that this child presents to you? Are you showering excessive attention on this youngster, at the expense of his/her siblings? Sort out your emotions and release and let go of any guilt, anger, frustration, sadness, fear, or shame. Replace them immediately with light and love. Negative feelings help neither you nor the youngster, but they do hurt your relationship with each other, and with the rest of your family.

If you blame yourself for the situation, *forgive yourself* immediately, using the affirmation that I have taught you. Then let it go. Guilt is toxic. It is also a waste of your precious energy, which is better channeled into loving support.

Avoid being judgmental. Accept the child and the situation as they are and start from there. Build a relationship with your offspring that will facilitate his or her need to learn. Nurture yourself and continue to be a loving parent to any other children you have. Ask the Creator for guidance to help you get through this, so that you may grow and heal from it.

HEALING IS A PROCESS THAT TAKES TIME

We are capable of healing. When you sustain a cut in a finger, doesn't that lesion heal, provided that you are in reasonably good health? The key is to let go of all the impediments to your recuperation. Focus on and visualize what you want rather than on whatever is not working. Make the decision to recover first, and then ask for healing, realizing that it may take place at the spiritual rather than the physical level.

We have the power to heal the *effects* of the past, but we cannot change what has happened. When we accept our mistakes as learning experiences, when we let go of the past and the loved ones who need to move on, then we can progress to the next encounter. In that way we speed up our recovery.

Healing takes place in the here and now. You cannot fix the past. Like water over the dam, it is gone forever. The future has not yet arrived, so why worry about things that have not yet happened? You can change your future, however, when you do something different in the present. When you do what you need to do to grow right here, right now, one moment at a time, you will actually *hasten your recovery.*

Healing starts with you. You can change *yourself,* with the help of the Creator. No one else can do it for you. You can *assist* others in their healing, however, by being supportive, by sharing your knowledge and skills, and most of all by loving in an unconditional manner. You can lighten their burden by sending them *love and light.* First, visualize light, then add your love, and then send them on their way, through the air. They will reach their recipients, no matter how far you may be from them. Love and light are forms of energy that can travel through space, just like the light from the stars or the sun. Thus you can *contribute to the healing* of loved ones, and all of humanity.

We have the ability to assist Grandmother Earth in restoring herself. We are part of her, and yet we are the perpetrators who keep injuring her. When we heal ourselves and keep grounding ourselves in her, we transmit our healing energy to her. Then Earth can *heal herself.*

TWELVE

Adult Children: Letting Go

You cared for me these many years;
Thank you for that.
My path is calling to me now.
I must depart.
Wherever I go, your love is there
And my love is with you.
I will return.

CONTINUING THE CONNECTION

The quality of your association with your offspring changes when they reach adulthood. If you fight that passage, if you continue to treat your grownup sons and daughters like children, you will hamper your further development as well as theirs; and that would create an unhealthy dependence, as well as imbalance, in your relationship. Tantamount to a lack of respect for your adult children, it would cost you their respect. You risk losing the very attributes that you want to retain: your children's trust, their good will, and their desire to spend time with you. When you let go of the need to parent, on the other hand, you will see the personalities of the young people unfold and come into their own. You will find a new way of relating to one another, one of equality and friendship, that will further growth for each of you.

Is it easy to let go of mothering and fathering habits? No, it is not. To complicate things, your needs change, as you enter a new phase of life yourself. New challenges make their appearance: accepting the fact that you are growing older; changes in your relationships with spouses, partners, friends; decisions regarding careers that cease to be satisfying; retirement, etc., etc. Add to that the need to let go of your offspring, and you will find that you are in a most demanding situation indeed. Isn't it great that you have accumulated all that maturity and life experience over the years, to help you get through this?

The traditional ways in which people cope at this point are escapist in nature. Some throw themselves into addictive behavior to anesthetize their pain and fears; others find themselves a lover; and some commit slow suicide with alcohol, nicotine, or other drugs. Many choose to bury themselves in work. The fact is that none of these escapes works for long. Indeed, their long term effects can be devastating to the individual and his or her environment. Let us then consider some less invasive methods that also happen to be much more effective. But first let's take a look at your needs.

MEETING YOUR OWN NEEDS

Perhaps you are going through a period of rapid transitions and spiritual growth spurts now, interspersed with soul searching and backtracking. Detours abound. You'll find out that there is no such thing as a straight line from point A to point B. Is it any wonder that you feel vulnerable, stressed, and fearful? Most likely you are having a grief reaction to all the changes in your life. This is a good time to review the section on dealing with grief in chapter 11. When you are ready, release and let go of your fears and other negative emotions.

It is crucial that you take care of yourself physically, mentally, emotionally, and spiritually. Be sure to get healthful nutrition and plenty of exercise. Keep stimulating yourself mentally; continue loving yourself unconditionally; and see to your spiritual needs. How do you do all of that?

Let's have a short review.

Loving and Nurturing Yourself

♥ Release and let go of negative feelings as quickly as you can.
♥ Replace them with love and light at once.
♥ Give thanks to the Creator for the growth experiences that your challenges provide.
♥ Meditate several times daily.
♥ Fill yourself with light, and surround yourself with it.
♥ Ground yourself in Grandmother Earth with nature walks and activities.
♥ Create new interests and recreational activities in your life.
♥ Keep challenging yourself.
♥ Write down your feelings and insights.

Emotional nurturing, and someone with whom you can share your feelings are helpful. There's no one in your life to do this for you? That is not really surprising. We expect our spouses, partners, friends, kids, to meet our needs, but how can they do that when they have their own to look after?

Turn to the Creator, who is always there, within you and around you. Surrender everything to Him. Do you remember that exercise that we did in a previous chapter, where you drop all your negative feelings into His great, loving hands?

Do it again, and then go into yourself. Remember that you are your own best friend. Nurture yourself, using the skills that I have taught you.

Make sure that you maintain balance between giving and receiving. When you give out more emotional support than you get back, you will drain yourself very quickly. Ask for assistance as you need it, and accept it, to even out the balance.

Get plenty of touching. If there is no one to do that for you, give yourself a hug, or get a teddy bear or other stuffed animal to hug. You might seek out massage therapy or reflexology to receive touch.

PETS ARE A WONDERFUL RESOURCE

Many people experience the companionship of animals as healing. Cats and dogs have the ability to love unconditionally. They will demonstrate that to you when you love them in that way too. If you adopt an abandoned pet, it may not trust you at first, however. Give it your love, and feelings of security and trust will develop in time.

Maggie, the cat whose human I am, adopted me when she was three years old. One day, as I was picking up the newspaper to read it, she took off in terror and raced to her hiding place! Guessing that someone must have beaten her with a paper, I dropped what I was doing and reassured her. Gradually, by telling her that I love her, showing her by my actions that she is safe with me, and never pushing myself on her, I earned her trust. Maggie is now very affectionate and showers me with love. She has taught me a great deal about unconditional loving.

Keep in mind that life is in perpetual motion. If you do not like what you are going through, take comfort in knowing that it will not last. Use the down-times for clearing out left-over negativity, emotionally and physically. You are what you believe. When you are convinced that only bad things happen to you, they will. When you give thanks for all that you receive daily, and focus on the good things that you want in your life, you will attract those.

MEDITATION

Meditation can help you release and let go. It will also enable you to dream your dreams, to visualize where you are going now. How do you do that? Let's check it out.

Dreaming Your Dream

1. Find a place to meditate. Make yourself comfortable.
2. Close your eyes.
3. Focus on your breathing as I taught you before.
4. Exhale whatever negativity you are ready to release.
5. Inhale the Creator's love for you.
6. Surround yourself with light, fill yourself with it.
7. Gently, **without forcing**, picture what you want to do now.
8. Make sure that it is for **your highest good.**
9. See yourself doing it. Surround the image with light.
10. When you are ready, open your eyes.
11. Write down your feelings and inspiration.

Did you find it difficult to do this exercise? If you wish to pursue this further, you might enroll in a class on meditation.

FILLING THE EMPTY NEST

For thousands of years, mankind has been practicing cutting the apron strings with children. If we have got any better with it, it certainly does not show up in our genes. For most of us it is still unsettling to let our children go. All our fears come to the fore. Can they really survive without our guidance? How will we ever get along in an empty nest? What will we talk about when the kids are gone? What will I do now to fill my time? Oh no, I'm getting old!

Let's go back to some of our relations, those that fly, the birds. In a previous chapter, we considered their nest building, as you may recall. What do they do when all the young have flown off into the sunrise? Do they stop singing? Usually, they simply return to whatever they were doing before their offspring came along. Perhaps that is something that you could learn to do as well. Pick up the life that you abandoned to concentrate on child rearing, and continue once more on your own path.

This might be a good time to go back to school, or to prepare yourself for that career that you really want. Or maybe you would like to start your own business. In other words, there is an opportunity here for you to do something for yourself. Create new challenges and interests for yourself. Perhaps you want to try being one of those volunteer parenting assistants that I mentioned in a previous chapter.

Do I hear you say "but I'm too old for all of this!"? Age is a state of mind. If you tell yourself that you are old, you will feel old. I went back to school and started my counseling career in mid-life. Maturity actually helped me in all my endeavors. Choose a field in which life experience and maturity are assets. That way, age will not be held against you.

Perhaps your marriage, or long term relationship, is in need of a tune-up. You have more time and energy for each other now. Invest it in fine tuning your kinship with each other. Work out old buried feelings with each other. Improve your communication. There are many workshops for couples that you can attend ~ ***together.*** Go for couples counseling if indicated.

As you implement my suggestions, you will find your energy increasing. Use that energy to have fun and to do those things that you have always been trying to get around to.

Now let us see how you can pursue a healthy relationship with your grown children.

BUILDING AN ADULT RELATIONSHIP WITH GROWN CHILDREN

You are still a parent, but your job description has changed. Your offspring have grown up. Recognize that they have their own life now. It is time to detach, to step back emotionally, with love. Hammer out a new role for yourself. Be a friend to your sons and daughters. Be loving and supportive, but avoid taking over. It is their responsibility to take care of themselves now and they are old enough to do it. Listen when they need a sounding board. Give advice when they ask for it, or when you see them heading for disaster.

Most likely the young peoples' values are different from yours. Avoid being critical or judgmental, even if you do not like their life style or choice of partner. Recognize their right to freedom of choice.

Open lines of communication are as important as ever. Use the feeling talk for expressing negative emotions that come up between you, always ending with I wish you would. Treat the young people with the same respect that you bestow on any adult. Continue to love them unconditionally. Give them hugs, and tell them I love you.

Some people live vicariously through their children. Cindy is widowed. Since her husband passed on, she has come to rely heavily on her son, Albert, even though she is only in her late fifties and in excellent health. She has no life of her own. Though Albert is married, she expects him to visit her every weekend. She then hangs on his every word, questioning him endlessly about everything that he is doing.

What kind of life is that? It's like watching a movie rather than being part of the action. What Cindy needs to do is to get herself a life and live it to the fullest.

HOW TO LIVE HAPPILY EVER AFTER

Actually it is easier to accomplish this than you might think. Let's start with fine-tuning your perception.

Toward Living Joyfully

1. Take a deep breath in and blink at your situation three times.
2. Now breathe out your negative feelings about it, and look at the situation again. Not so bad any more, is it?
3. In your journal, write down one thing that you have always wanted to do "if only I had the time!" You have the time now.
4. Write down how you are going to put step 3 into action; add any fears that might stop you.
5. Start taking that action as soon as possible. Then write down your feelings about taking this step.

Do I hear you say that you cannot be joyful? Think again! We all have the power to be happy. How old do you have to be to give yourself permission to use yours? Living in joy is a choice. It does not just happen. Of course you have the freedom to live miserably, if that is your will. But then at least enjoy your misery!

THE TAPESTRY OF LIFE

To me life is like a tapestry, one of those huge ones that you see hanging in museums. I weave mine, and you weave yours. Everything that has ever happened to us shows up in our tapestries. The past is there, the present is about to find its way into them, the future has not yet made it. Everything is just there, no regrets. And nothing that is in them can be removed or changed. Like any artist or weaver, I have control over what goes into my work of art, however. So I have become very careful in my choices. I want my tapestry to be a true reflection of who I am, you see. What do you want yours to be?

Can you weave the future into your tapestry? Quite difficult, isn't it, for it has not yet happened. Then why are so many of us dwelling in the future? The here and now is where we can make a difference. So live in the present, one day at a time, to the fullest. **And enjoy!**

THIRTEEN

The Power of Love

What drives the universe,
Holds galaxies in place,
Propels our Earth,
Makes flowers grow?

What moves the Spirit
Through all creation,
What is this force
That binds together
The great All?
It is love,
It's always been love!
Love is the power,
Love is the juice
Of life itself!

LOVE AS HEALER

Unconditional love is so gentle that its power is often overlooked or underestimated. Yet it is incredibly potent. It is a change agent unlike any other. When we practice it daily, we heal ourselves spiritually and facilitate recovery in others; we purify our living space here on Grandmother Earth; and we guide our children properly, passing along to them the ability to love that way too. Moreover, we fulfill our contract with the Creator, which is to bring His love and Light to the part of the universe that we inhabit.

HEALING YOURSELF

When you open your heart to the Creator, His love flows into it unimpeded. When you love yourself, you can hear Him speak to you through your heart or through His messengers. From then on, you will refuse to be a vessel for negative beliefs or feelings; you will no longer grant them rent-free space inside you. When you release those beliefs and emotions and let them go, as you continue to love yourself without conditions, you will uncover your true self. In other words, you will find yourself healing at the spirit or soul level, the only site where true recovery takes place.

As you heal, you will no longer be comfortable living and working in situations that are filled with negativity. You will close the doors on them, and as you do so, you will see others, that you did not even know existed, open up. Once you walk through them, one by one, you will behold more clearly the numerous options available to you. Continuing to listen to your inner voice, and allowing yourself to be led by it, you will discover your path, your true purpose. When you heed the call to follow it, things will start falling into place. Then you will know that you are on the right course for you.

How do I know all of this? I know, because I have been there. I have gone through it all myself, step by step. This process does not happen overnight, however. Being a journey, it may take months, it may last years. For example, I could not write this book until I had walked the walk and had grown sufficiently to understand its message myself. Once I was there, it just flowed through me and on to you.

To illustrate, let me share with you what transpired when I sat down to write this chapter. Nothing, nada! Do you know what that means to a writer, when we have nothing to say? Oh, I squeezed out a few words, but then I stopped in frustration. Catching myself, I realized that this was not the time, that I was not ready to put on paper whatever needed to be written. So I laid the manuscript aside to do some more growing. I asked for guidance. I walked through the circle of healing, that I am about to share with you. Then I went to sleep for the night. When I woke up in the morning, I tried again. The words came tumbling out once more, so fast that I could hardly keep up with them. The next day, before I could start writing, I was guided to walk the circle again.

Your growth will take whatever amount of time is just right for you, gentle reader. So be calm. Patience is not only a virtue. It is a skill that we must learn in order to proceed on our path. When I get impatient, I remind myself that the Creator's clock is not set to Earth time. In working with Him, we truly have all of eternity. Is that time enough for you?

When we embark on a trip, we like to have a map to guide us. So why not take along a chart for this all-important journey? The one that I have prepared for you looks different from the everyday road map. Life, like Grandmother Earth, is round. As you have already experienced, there are few straight lines from one destination to another. So I have drawn up for you a map that shows the *Four Directions within the Circle of Spiritual Healing.* It is based on the teaching of Fire Lame Deer and Helene Sarkis in *The Lakota Sweat Lodge Cards.* The Lakota and other Native American Nations and Tribes remind us that the directions of the West, the North, the East, and the South teach us important lessons about life. Each has special messages for us on our pilgrimage here on Earth, as indicated below. You may use this guide daily to help you proceed on your path, and to pilot children on theirs.

THE CIRCLE IN LOVE AND HEALING

In the beginning of this book, I described the self-reinforcing cycle of parent-child stress. I went on to demonstrate, throughout these pages, how that cycle can be broken by replacing fear and other negative feelings with love. Now I will show you, in graphic fashion, how that works.

Like life, love and spiritual healing take place in a never-ending circle. You can walk that circle as often as you need to. Always start with the releasing and letting go of your negative feelings and beliefs.

A good place to carry out this exercise is in salt water. You will need a tub in which you can immerse yourself, and sea salt, which is available at health food stores. If you prefer, and have the opportunity, you can do this exercise in the sea as well.

Fill the tub with water of a temperature that is comfortable for you. You will be spending about fifteen minutes in it. Stir in two handfuls of sea salt until it is dissolved. Get into the tub when you are ready.

Caution: If you cannot tolerate tub baths or sea salt, this method is not for you at this time. Consult your health care practitioner before you attempt it.

The Four Directions Within
The Circle of Spiritual Healing
With Unconditional Love

ENLIGHTENMENT/WISDOM/GUIDANCE

WEST

PURIFICATION
RELEASING/LETTING GO

EAST

SUPPORT/INSPIRATION
BALANCE/HARMONY

GROWTH
ACCEPTANCE/LOVE/JOY

Based on Chief Archie Fire Lame Deer and Helene Sarkis, *the Lakota Sweat Lodge Cards*, Destiny Books, Rochester, VT, 1994

THE FOUR DIRECTIONS WITHIN THE CIRCLE OF SPIRITUAL HEALING WITH UNCONDITIONAL LOVE

1. Start in the position of the West. Sit or recline in the water. Make yourself comfortable. Close your eyes. Give thanks and ask for guidance with purification or cleansing, releasing, and letting go. Talk to your body. Thank it for carrying your spirit, for being there for you always. Tell it that you love it. Ask it to release the negative beliefs and feelings that you no longer need or want. Then say, "I am releasing and letting go of . . ."plugging in feelings and beliefs that you no longer need or want, one at a time. See them flow into the water. Notice how that feels.

2. The second stop is in the position of the North. Give thanks and ask for enlightenment, and wisdom. Relaxing in the salt water, picture light in whatever color presents itself to you. Invite the light to flow into you and fill first all those places from which you have released

negativity, then your entire self. Visualize it doing that. Ask for continuing guidance. How does that feel?

3. The third stop is in the position of the East. Give thanks and ask for support, new inspiration, and guidance in balancing and grounding yourself. Sitting or lying in the water, see yourself connected to Grandmother Earth. Picture yourself being in her womb, joined to her through a cord that flows from your body into her. Her water surrounds and supports you. She feeds you and clothes you, she sustains your body. Let this come fully to your consciousness. Let yourself feel the sense of balance and harmony that arises out of that awareness. Thank her and tell her that you love her.

4. The fourth stop is in the position of the South. Express your gratitude and ask for growth, acceptance, and joy. Become aware of your love for yourself and all our relations. Feel the spirit of the Creator moving through you and all of creation. Give thanks to Him for His love and guidance. Pat yourself on the back for all the effort that you are putting into your growth. Give thanks for this experience.

5. Rinse off with a cleansing shower. Step out of the tub, dry yourself, and dress in comfortable clothing or wrap yourself in a blanket.

6. Meditate on your experience, listening to your inner voice.

7. Write your reactions, feelings, and insights.

This exercise shows how the Creator uses unconditional love to help us purify, enlighten, and balance ourselves so that we may once again enter a state of harmony, love, and joy that enables us to continue growing spiritually. Yes, you can do it too. It might require some practice, so please be patient.

You may find yourself repeating these steps many times as you cleanse yourself of negatives. After you release and let go, you may have a physical reaction, including any or all of the following: increased perspiration and urination, diarrhea, even having to get up several times at night for this process of elimination. This is your body's way of releasing. It may last some time, depending upon how much negativity you have stored away. Once your body gets used to this regimen, it will want you to release and let go of negatives as soon as you become aware of them. Go with that, do not hold them in. You will feel better! And you will have more energy for fun.

WE CAN ASSIST GRANDMOTHER EARTH IN HER HEALING

It really starts with you and me. Yes, each one of us is that important. When you and the members of your family love each other, unconditionally, your whole family will mend. When families recuperate in our villages and towns, cities, states, and nations, people all over the globe will heal spiritually. You see, recovery is contagious. Once humanity is renewed, Grandmother Earth, the patient one who bears all our burdens, all our abuse, too will heal.

This is the power of love which we all share. We need to choose to accept it, however. We are channels of love and light for the Creator, but He has given us freedom of choice. If each of us takes the step to love unconditionally, all of us together will light up the night and will soon be dancing with joy on a healed planet.

WHAT ABOUT THE CHILDREN?

Adults are responsible for passing love along to children. When we love and respect them, our offspring learn to love and respect us and each other. It really *is* that simple. It follows that they learn to honor and respect themselves, the Creator, and all his creation. Would they ever want to harm that which they honor and love? Isn't that what love is all about?

When we parent with love, both ourselves and our children, we plant the seed of the greatest phenomenon that there is: love. This is the force that drives the universe, that holds everything in its assigned place, makes everything grow, and moves the spirit through it all. It is more powerful than anything that mankind ever created, because it comes from the Creator. Fathers and mothers and all members of the human community have the opportunity to participate in His creation by this one act, loving Him, themselves, and one another.

FULFILLING OUR CONTRACT WITH THE CREATOR

Now is the time to stop trying to change each other, to cease judging one another. Not only are you hurting the recipient with this treatment, you are also wasting your time and effort. For only the Creator or we ourselves can speed up our progress. So, lend a loving hand to those who need your support. Be a messenger of love and light by means of your example. Once enough of us participate in this creative act within the circle of our families, friends, and neighbors, love will flow from grass root to grass root like an unstoppable flood.

Let us encourage each other with patience and understanding, while we each follow our own path through life. When we love unconditionally and accept ourselves and each other as we are and where we are on our journey, we fulfill your contract with the Creator.

WHAT IS LOVE?

Unconditional love is the life force itself. It is the Qi of Chinese tradition; it is the Kundalini of Hindu culture. Always around us, it is available to us wherever we are. Once we open our hearts to it, this kind of love protects and guides us, because it comes from the Creator. Once we turn away from it, we abandon the light and the Creator. The effects, as you see all around you, are disastrous. But though we might misplace it, love never gets lost. Its power is such that we can always return to it, we can always start over. It is never too late. For this kind of love knows no restriction, no condition. It just is, whether we know it or acknowledge it or not.

Gentle reader, we have come to the end of this volume. I hope, however, that this will be a new beginning for you. You are invited, by the Creator Himself, to step into the light, to join the dance, and let love flow through you to all creation.

For we are

Voices in the dark,

We bring love, we bring light

Into the night.

Dancing toward the light,

We lead all

Out of night.

Walk in peace, with love and light!

READING RESOURCES

The works listed below have influenced me and helped me grow. My thanks to their authors! I invite you to explore these books at any of our libraries or bookstores. If you find yourself drawn to other writings, go with the impulse. Let your intuition guide you. And enjoy!

I. Healing Yourself

Bradshaw, John, *Healing the Shame That Binds You*, 1988, Health Communications, Inc., Deerfield Beach, FL.

Ibid, *The Family*, 1988, Health Communications, Inc., Deerfield Beach, FL.

Capacchione, Lucia, PhD, *Recovery of Your Inner Child*, 1991, Simon & Schuster, New York.

Epstein, Donald M., DC, *The 12 Stages Of Healing*, 1994, Amber-Allen Publishing and New World Library, San Rafael, CA.

Epstein, Gerald, MD, *Healing Into Immortality*, 1994, Bantam Books, New York.

Hay, Louise L., *You Can Heal Your Life*, 1987, Hay House, Santa Monica, CA.

Osherson, Samuel, PhD, *Wrestling With Love*, 1992, Fawcett Columbine, New York.

Louden, Jennifer, *The Woman's Comfort Book*, 1992, Harper Collins Publishers, New York.

Secunda, Victoria, *Women and Their Fathers*, 1992, Delacorte Press, New York.

Tanner, Ira J., *Healing the Pain Of Everyday Loss*, 1976, Winston Press, Minneapolis, MN.

Whitfield, Charles L., MD., *Healing the Child Within*, 1987, Health Communications, Inc., Deerfield Beach, FL.

II. Growing Spiritually

Anderson, Sherry Ruth, & Hopkins, Patricia, *the Feminine Face of God*, 1991, Bantam Books, New York.

Bear Heart, with Molly Harkin, *The Wind Is My Mother*, 1996, Clarkson Potter/Publishers, New York.

Chief Archie Fire Lame Deer and Helene Sarkis, *The Lakota Sweat Lodge Cards*, Spiritual Teachings of The Sioux, 1994, Destiny Books, Rochester, VT.

Dreher, Diane, *the Tao Of Inner Peace*, 1990, HarperCollins Publishers, New York.

McFadden, Steven, *Ancient Voices, Current Affairs*, 1992, Bear & Company, Santa Fe, NM.

McGaa, Ed, Eagle Man, *Mother Earth Spirituality*, 1990, HarperCollins Publishers, New York.

Ibid, *Rainbow Tribe*, 1992, HarperCollins Publishers, New York.

Taylor, Terry Lynn, *Messengers of Light*, 1990, H.J. Kramer Inc., Tiburon, CA.

The Bible and *New Testament* in any of their numerous editions and publications.

III. Coupling

Comfort, Alex, *The Joy Of Sex*, 1972, Crown Publications, New York.

Wells, Carol G., *Right Brain Sex*, 1989, Prentice Hall Press, New York.

Wile, Daniel B., *After the Honeymoon*, 1988, John Wiley & Sons, Inc., New York.

IV. Guiding Children

Becker, Wesley, PhD *Parents Are Teachers, 1971*, Research Press, Champaign, IL.

Hamilton, Eleanor, PhD, *Sex, With Love*, 1978, Beacon Press, Boston.

Nelsen, Jane, and Lott, Lynn, *I'm on Your Side*, 1990, Prima Publishing & Communications, Rocklin, CA.

Ross, Stan, *Transforming Our Schools*, 2010, Stan Ross, 138 River Avenue, Mishawaka IN 46544

Turecki, Stanley, MD, with Wernick, Sarah, PhD, *the Emotional Problems of Normal Children*, 1994, Bantam Books, New York.